you&**your**

Jaguar **XK8**

you & your
Jaguar XK8

Nigel Thorley *Buying, enjoying, maintaining, modifying*

First published in 2006

Nigel Thorley has asserted his right to
be identified as the author of this work

British Library Cataloguing-in-Publication Data:
A catalogue record for this book is available
from the British Library

ISBN 1 84425 224 8

Library of Congress catalog card no. 2005935260

Published by Haynes Publishing,
Sparkford, Yeovil, Somerset BA22 7JJ, UK
Tel: 01963 442030 Fax: 01963 440001
Int. tel: +44 1963 442030 Int. fax: +44 1963 440001
E-mail: sales@haynes.co.uk
Website: www.haynes.co.uk

Haynes North America, Inc.,
861 Lawrence Drive, Newbury Park,
California 91320, USA

Designed by G&M Designs Limited,
Raunds, Northamptonshire
Printed and bound in Great Britain by
J. H. Haynes & Co. Ltd, Sparkford

Contents

Acknowledgements

Having written two previous 'You and Your' titles on Jaguar models, this type of publication seems an ideal vehicle (pardon the pun) to explore a particular car, whether for those generally interested in the model or those who have such a car and want to learn more.

Though working on a publication involving such a comparatively modern vehicle as the XK8 would seem, at first, to be relatively easy, with its history and development being 'uncoloured' by the passage of time, that is certainly not the case. It would not have been possible for me to write this book without a great deal of help from many people, and I apologise to any that I miss in this brief acknowledgement.

Firstly, of course, I must thank Jaguar Cars Limited, who designed, built and sold the cars in the first place. The car was in production for under ten years, yet the changes, modifications, model revisions, etc, were numerous, so I am fortunate that Jaguar were able to provide me with access to their records, and allow me to use them freely. Allied to this were the services provided by the Jaguar Daimler Heritage Trust, the charitable organisation set up by Jaguar to secure and maintain their archive for posterity. Their resource is immense and extremely useful to authors like myself.

Many thanks also go to Jaguar independent technician David Marks, whose wealth of knowledge on modern Jaguars is unsurpassed; a technical expert for the Jaguar Enthusiasts Club, he provided a great deal of assistance in the preparation of the purchase and maintenance chapters of this book.

The Jaguar Enthusiasts Club itself also played an important part. The largest Jaguar club in the world, it offers immense support to owners and enthusiasts of the XK models and has formed a special XK8 Model Forum through which members can communicate on all matters relating to these cars. This too has proved a valuable source of research material.

Thanks also go to Mark Hughes of Haynes Publishing, who first thought up the idea of this and the other titles in the 'You and Your' series. His foresight spurred me on in writing this important book about these fine Jaguar sports cars.

Last, but not least, I have to thank my wife Pauline as usual, for putting up with my consistent and obsessive involvement with the Jaguar marque. It is fortunate that she loves our own XK8!

Nigel Thorley
March 2006

Introduction

The background and history of the Jaguar marque has been adequately documented many times before in other more detailed publications than this. Suffice to say at this point that the original business (the Swallow Sidecar Company) commenced operation in the town of Blackpool in England in 1922, as a partnership between William Walmsley and William Lyons.

The business eventually moved on to produce stylish bodies on existing motor car chassis, primarily for Austin, later for Morris, Standard and many others, which resulted in the company relocating to Coventry in Warwickshire, the heart of the British motor industry.

In 1932 they produced the SS1 two door Coupé. Not only was this the first use of the 'SS' brand name – later to be changed to Jaguar, after the Second World War – but it was also the company's first in-house designed car. Interestingly, it set the scene for the future development of other two-door models which eventually led to the XK8, the subject of this publication.

The five generations of Jaguar production sports cars – from the rear forwards, 1930s SS100; 1948–61, XK120 (including XK140 and XK150); 1961–74, E-type Series 1 (also Series 2 and 3); 1975–96, XJS and XK8 (including XKR), 1996–2005. (Nigel Thorley collection)

By the late 1930s the company's emphasis had switched to saloons (now carrying the title 'SS Jaguar'), plus a small-production-run rakish sports car, the SS100 and, after the War, the XK120. This latter, highly successful two-seater was updated in the 1950s to become the XK140 and 150, before ending production in 1961 to make way for the next generation of Jaguar sports car, the legendary E-type. The E-type remained in production for a total of 13 years, and during that time a 2+2 version appeared, a reflection of the need then, as now, for extra seating in a sports car.

When the E-type finally met its demise, Jaguar, like many other manufacturers, turned their attention to 'grand touring' cars, still sporting in nature but with extra seating within a two-door arrangement and providing supreme comfort within a quality and performance package. From the then superb XJ saloon, the XJ-S was born in 1975.

Unloved at first, mainly due to its avant-garde styling, the XJ-S grew in both stature and quality over an enforced production run amounting to 21 years, during which time Jaguar went through its troubled British Leyland era, leading almost to oblivion, then privatisation and revitalisation, and finally to Ford ownership in 1989. Ford spent £1.6 billion buying Jaguar, paying off its debts, dealing with redundancies, and putting the product quality right.

Prior to all this, in 1980 the Italian coachbuilder Pininfarina had shown its concept Jaguar Spyder, achieving a contemporary interpretation of the 1960s E-type. This sparked Jaguar's own development project, leading up to the Ford takeover, of what it thought would be the eventual XJS replacement model, coded XJ41, to become known as the 'F-type' – which Ford duly assigned to the scrapheap.

Eventually, utilising Ford money and advances in technology, a new Jaguar, codenamed the X-100, was launched in 1996 as the XK8. The rest, as they say, is history, and is fully reported herein. It was a great achievement for Jaguar at the time, and remains a car that has stood the test of time against stiff competition from other manufacturers, and has only recently been replaced by another technologically advanced model that, in tribute to its predecessor, also carries the insignia 'XK'.

This publication tells the story of the XK8, its development and its pros and cons, and hides nothing from those who own, are contemplating the purchase of, or are just interested in reading about these superb cars.

Chapter One

X-100 to XK8 in under five years

Background to change

Jaguar were well known for the longevity of their models and designs – take the XK120, for instance, launched in 1948, which in its last (XK150) form was still around in 1961. But even by Jaguar standards the XJ-S was getting a bit long in the tooth by the end of the 1980s.

The constant upgrading and modification of an existing product can sometimes cost as much as, if not more than, starting with a clean sheet of paper, so for some considerable time Jaguar engineers had been working on an entirely new sports car project to eventually replace the XJ-S. This was codenamed XJ41, later to be known as the F-type.

Loosely based on the XJ6 (coded XJ40) – the saloon car range already under development and finally introduced in 1986 – the XJ41 used that vehicle's floorpan, AJ6 engine and transmission. Later developments included a turbocharged engine, four-wheel drive, and a convertible version (coded XJ42). But ideas constantly changed, money was short, development was stunted by the redirection of resources to the saloon cars, and there appeared to be little co-ordination between the people involved in the project. Eventually it became a standalone project distinct from the XJ40, which made it even more expensive. By this time it was overweight and would have under-performed, and it just didn't gel as a viable successor to Jaguar's sporting car line.

By the time XJ41 was a drivable vehicle ready for evaluation it had become clear that it had out-stayed

Various examples of XJ41 (the stillborn Jaguar F-type sports car project) that never made it to production. (JDHT)

The Convertible XJ41 in its final form, displaying elements of US rear styling. (JDHT)

its welcome: it was cramped and uncompetitive in the market place that had developed by that time. Then, after the Ford takeover of Jaguar in 1989, the project was scrapped (writing off about £15 million of work), although elements of the styling eventually found their way back in the form of the Aston Martin DB7.

John Egan (at the helm of Jaguar prior to the Ford takeover) had done a remarkable job bringing the company back from the brink after the British Leyland era. Overall quality had improved, money exchange rates had helped profitability, privatisation had boosted morale, and the XJ40 resulted in world record Jaguar sales in 1988 and 1989 that wouldn't be exceeded again until 1998.

Jaguar's first new Ford boss, Bill Hayden, re-emphasised the goals set previously by John Egan. Even better build quality would be vital if Jaguar was to stay in existence. After the despatch of an XJ40 saloon to the States for Ford to review, strip and evaluate, it was clear that although Jaguar had made great strides since the early 1980s, there was still a great deal of

The final interior layout of the XJ41 showed a lack of finesse to the styling and certainly less legroom and headroom than in an XJS. (JDHT)

work to do. Fortunately, this led to improvements in the design and reputation of cars like the XJ-S, at that time still Jaguar's only sporting model and destined for an elongated lifespan beyond its sell-by date.

Ford's first priority as far as new cars was concerned, however, was the saloon car range, because that was where the volume sales, and therefore the profits, were to be found. Although the XJ40 was still in essence a good car, it had to be brought up to date if Jaguar was not to suffer a set-back against ever stiffer competition. Hence the X-300 project was born, Ford's input helping Jaguar build a substantially better car, with a return to more curvaceous styling. The 'heritage' card also came into play, as the new saloon not only looked like previous XJs but was carefully marketed as such.

The X-300 was a tribute to what Ford had brought to the Jaguar table, and to the Jaguar design team that had been able to make so many improvements in so short a time, as it went into production in 1994, under four years after its inception. It showed the world, and the company's Ford bosses, that Jaguar were still a viable company producing great cars.

Development of a new sports car

With work on the X-300 saloon coming along nicely by 1991, thoughts turned to what would be the next new project. Would it be an upgrade to the existing XJ-S, at this time still selling well; a completely new replacement; or another, perhaps smaller, saloon? As we now know, the first stage was to commit £50 million to a facelift of the XJ-S (thereafter known as the

The XJ41 Coupé shows design elements of the XJ220 and XK8 at the front. (JDHT)

XJS), which appeared that year. This gave Jaguar time to consider its future plans.

Bob Dover, a relatively late arrival at Jaguar from Land Rover, was appointed head of the Sports Car Team. It was very late in 1991 that a decision was taken to look to an XJS replacement, even though finance would continue to be a major problem and there was no commitment from

The X-300 (XJ6, seen here in XJR supercharged form) was a tremendous step forward and brought a lot to the table in terms of the XK8 sports car. (Nigel Thorley collection)

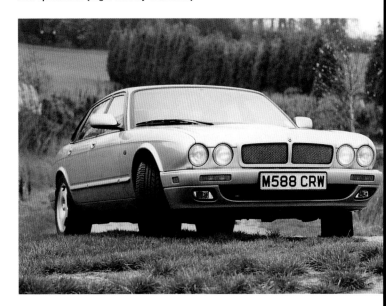

BOB DOVER

Bob Dover started his career in mechanical engineering, becoming an apprentice at Farnborough in 1962, and in 1968 he joined British Leyland as a project engineer. By 1978 he was working for tractor manufacturers Massey-Fergusson, and then in 1988 he moved to Land Rover as Director of Manufacturing. He joined Jaguar in 1990 as Director of Manufacturing, New Products, and in 1992 became head of the X-100 team as Chief Programme Engineer, Sports Cars. He later moved over to Aston Martin.

GEOFF LAWSON

Born in Leicester, the brilliant stylist Geoff Lawson studied design and took a Masters degree in furniture design at the Royal College of Art. He joined Vauxhall Motors in 1969 as a designer and worked on car and truck programmes in Europe and the US for General Motors, progressing to Chief Designer level. He was appointed Jaguar's Director of Styling in 1984. His work with Jaguar included the facelifted XJS, the X-300 saloon, the XJ220 supercar, the New Series XJ saloons, and the XK8. Geoff died suddenly in June 1999 at the age of 54.

Ford to approve such a project – a situation that would continue for some considerable time.

Feeling that a fresh outlook was needed (as the XJS was very much a grand touring car rather than an out-and-out sports car like it's predecessor, the E-type), the marketing strategy for the proposed 'new' model would change, because the 'S' had never been as popular in the valued US market as the E-type had been in its day.

1992: work begins

Bob Dover's Sports Car Team was made up of a mere 24 people, including Jaguar's Chief Stylist Geoff

Lawson. They had to work to a very strict brief to produce an entirely new Jaguar sports car to a relatively minor (and at the time somewhat theoretical) budget of £300 million, which had to accommodate an existing floorpan and a new AJ26 engine, yet to be built.

A further facelift to the XJS was considered, which would have been economical and would have provided a quick-fix, even to the point of grafting on an X-300 look-alike front, but it was inevitable that

Interesting styling alternatives for the XJS considered as a stopgap until an entirely new sports car could be produced. (JDHT)

96.5 MY XJS

styling cues from the E-type or even the XJ220 supercar would have to be considered. Although the concept of reviving the XJS didn't go away for quite some time, Jaguar finally committed to the preparation of designs and the building of four clay models to evaluate the possibilities for an entirely new car, coded X-100.

External styling

Geoff Lawson assigned Fergus Pollock as X-100 Project Leader, and they commissioned four clay models to be created for evaluation. This coincided with Bill Hayden's retirement from the company. He was replaced at the helm of Jaguar by Nick Scheele, another ex-Ford man who had run their Mexican operation. He arrived at a crucial time in the early days of the X-100 project, with great enthusiasm for both the car and the company.

As well as two in-house designs from Jaguar's Whitley Engineering facility, Geoff enlisted the help of Ford's own styling department in the US, as well as their Italian coachbuilding subsidiary, Ghia. The results were ready in March of 1992 and were based on four specific themes, entitled 'Evocative, Radical, Progressive and Evolutionary'. At this point only the

Coupé was being worked on, Geoff Lawson considering that this was the most vital design to get right and that the Convertible would more easily follow from it.

Clay No. 1: Evolutionary design

This was a design created externally for Jaguar by Moray Callum, a Ghia designer, the brother of Ian Callum of Aston Martin and now Jaguar fame. Based on the concept of a traditional luxury GT design to appeal to existing XJS type customers, the 'evolutionary' aspects of the design would, hopefully, also appeal to new customers enticed away from Jaguar's competition.

A relatively pretty design, although somewhat slab-sided, it bore some resemblance to a Porsche 911 yet retained a touch of Jaguar traditionalism with an oval grille, not too dissimilar to earlier Jaguar models and, in hindsight, remarkably close to the S-type saloon grille from 1999. With a very large rear screen, and an enormous and severely tapered rear end, this clay got through the initial assessment in March but was abandoned next time around in June.

Clay No. 2: Radical design

This was an in-house design created by Jaguar's team at their relatively new Whitley Engineering Division in Coventry. One of several designs worked on by Keith

Clay No. 2 emphasising just how radical this design was for Jaguar then, as it would still be now. (JDHT)

Helfet (one of the few engineers and designers at Jaguar who had worked under Sir William Lyons, the founder of the company) and his boss Geoff Lawson, this was to be an avant-garde, almost adventurous design, to get a feel for how far Jaguar could go within contemporary design.

With a pronounced windscreen, Porsche-style doors, no rear side windows, a roofline somewhat reminiscent of a TVR Cerbera, and a severe rear overhang and taper, this was moving right away from anything Jaguar had done before. Nevertheless, the front end sported a grille somewhat resembling that of the racing C-types of the 1950s.

This Radical concept was also carried over to the next review in June.

Clay No. 3: Progressive design

The second non-Jaguar design, created for them by Ford in the US, was derived from the XJS. It again used the oval style of radiator grille but with frontal lighting not too distant from what would eventually be the XK8 design. From the side this concept was decidedly XJS in the lower section, and even the door aperture owed much to the old car. At the rear were a very large tailgate and a rear window with an unusual lighting technique. An interesting detail was the use of bumper bar blades, a feature to appear

Another styling exercise that enjoyed a short stay of execution. (JDHT)

later on cars like the S-type and many competitors' vehicles.

This concept was out of favour at the first viewing in March 1992.

Revised Clay No. 2 design was, however, also later abandoned. (JDHT)

Clay No. 3 was heavily derived from the XJS, though from this angle it has a distinct Porsche 911 look to the side rear. This clay was ruled out very early on. (JDHT)

Clay No. 4: Evocative design

The second of the Jaguar Whitley concepts, this was designed to create a style echoing previous Jaguar sporting car successes like the XK120 and E-type. Meant to appeal to a younger audience but not to be so contemporary as to put off existing XJS or other Jaguar owners, it also used a traditional radiator grille but of smaller dimensions and with a

Clay No. 4, an in-house design that it was felt had the greatest promise from which to generate another clay. (JDHT)

prominent centre rib (à la the Mark 2 of the 1960s). With concealed headlights, the bonnet line and auxiliary lighting features would later be seen in the 'real' XK8. The side view also showed touches of the final car, and they retained the rear quarter-windows with a nicely sloping roof section. At the rear there was still a lot of work to do, obviously. Note the return of the centrally mounted exhaust pipes (à la E-type).

Along with the other Whitley design, this concept carried over to the next stage in June, by which time the designs had gone through the various stages of their viability studies.

After another review mid year it was Clay No. 4 (the Whitley Evocative concept) that was chosen for further development, although it was decided that another clay model should be produced to move the theme forward. This became known, confusingly, as Clay A (for 'Alternative').

Enter Clay A

Much better proportioned than Clay 4, this design was shorter. It featured sculptured sill and rear valance areas not unlike the XJ220 supercar and even had a

This was Clay No. 4 at a later stage in development, by this time renamed Clay M. Clear signs of XJ220 and the eventual XK8 are coming through at the front, but although not noticeable in this view it still had a very pronounced rear overhang. (JDHT)

Clay A, and the XK8 as we know it takes shape. With its shortened rear overhang and tidy up of the frontal view, this is now very close to the final design, though the front wing curvature still has to be altered, as does the door style and form. (JDHT)

Another angle of Clay A, showing its very close relationship to the final car from the rear. The idea of a differently coloured rear bumper lasted for a while. Also note the addition of a badge on the boot lid, which did not appear in production form until the original XKR model. (JDHT)

nose not too distinct from the old E-type and the newer XJ220. Geoff Lawson, Jaguar's own stylist, had a strong belief in what Jaguar was all about, and felt that the heritage of Sir William's style should not be ignored, and this was apparent in this concept. Although there was still lots of work to do, the XK8 was now beginning to appear.

Interior Design A was too traditional for the new Jaguar sports car. (JDHT)

Interior design

Work on the interior design and layout of the new car went on alongside the external styling. Care had to be taken not to upset existing buyers who loved Jaguar's well known traditional touches of leather and wood, nor to be too outrageous and get sucked into the world of gadgetry. Five possible choices were arrived at for consideration, of which half-sized models were produced.

Design A: Traditional

This was indeed quite traditional, and was to be saloon car-derived in order to provide good parts interchangeability – indeed, some of these styling features found their way into the later X-308 (XJ8 saloons) launched in 1997. It was a good 'safe' design but was not sporty enough for the X-100 strategy, so was abandoned.

Design B: Progressive

This design had an enlarged sweeping centre console design. The passenger side was devoid of any detail while the instrument pack ahead of the driver was obviously derived from a Ford Scorpio. At the time this design was considered a good base to work from, but more design choice was requested. Although abandoned, areas like the centre console seem to have later found favour in the Aston Martin DB7.

Interior Design B was what Jaguar termed 'Progressive'. It was ultimately deemed unsuitable – and just look at those door trims! (JDHT)

Design C: Evolutionary

Trying to achieve a halfway compromise between the traditional and the new, this design incorporated loads of woodwork and a somewhat squat centre console area. It was ruled out in the first review in March 1992.

Interior Design C was still traditional in the dashboard layout, acres of wood on the door trims and unusual shaping to the centre console area. (JDHT)

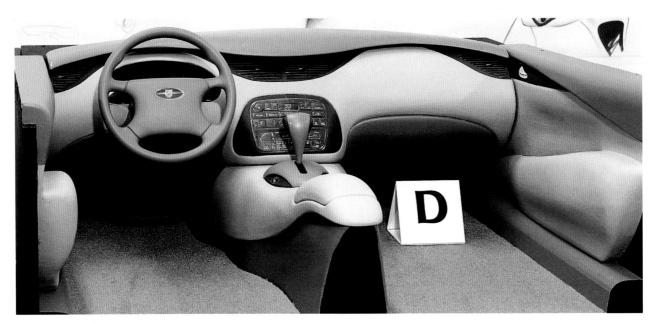

Interior Design D, which seemed – even to the layman's eye – to have nothing favourable about it. (JDHT)

Design D: Avant-garde

This was like nothing Jaguar had ever tried before. With no wood and somewhat featureless details, it received the thumbs down right from the start and was instantly rejected.

Design E: Radical

This was to be Jaguar's radical alternative with sweeping curves everywhere, no pronounced centre

The 'Radical' Design E interior concept, which was just that! (JDHT)

console area at all, and a definitely American influence to many features.

Not convinced that these concepts were the way forward, in June 1992 more choices were provided in the form of sketches, and one particular example found favour. With a full-width veneered dashboard with curved top, this became known as the 'Spitfire wing' design. Although it was indeed very traditional – particularly so in the original drawing, which seems to have taken some cues from much earlier cars, like the 1950s Bristols – a later derivation in October was more subtle and was adopted for further development.

From this point it didn't take long for the final style to emerge, with the main instruments in front of the driver and ancillary gauges in the centre section above an X-300-derived centre console area. The choice of dashboard 'finish' came up for review and no less than nine types were focus tested across the world – everything from traditional walnut veneer, through grey stained wood, brushed aluminium, carbon fibre and even Chinese lacquer. At the time it was only the walnut and grey staining that proved popular, and these finishes were finally agreed for the early cars.

During 1992 Jaguar carried out some major market research by organising focus groups. The one held in the US was shown pictures of the various designs, while a later one held at the National Exhibition Centre in Birmingham was shown the modified Clay 4 (now confusingly renamed Clay M), displayed alongside Clay A, the existing XJS, and the competition from other manufacturers like Mercedes. On the latter occasion a specially chosen audience of 300 potential customers for such cars was selected for a detailed evaluation of the vehicles. Perhaps not surprisingly both the new Jaguar proposals were rated equally highly, although Clay A (more akin to the eventual final design) rated better in Convertible form than Coupé.

The first mock-up of what would eventually be the XK8 dash layout. (JDHT)

Six days after this focus group – by which time all the results had been evaluated – Jaguar finally sanctioned Clay A, although it must be emphasised that even at this point Ford had not given approval for the project to go into final development and production. With the final external design agreed, outside consultants could now digitise the styling model to create a fibreglass representation for final detailing. Two such cars were built for various show purposes, but neither were runners at this stage.

The Jaguar team were now fired up over the X-100 project under the ultimate leadership of Nick Scheele and other key personnel, the only major problem being that Ford had still not given their global approval to

November 1992, and *Autocar* were on the trail of the new Jaguar. (Reprinted from *Autocar* magazine)

finance it. However, Ford themselves were at the same time developing their own new Mustang, so the interchange of ideas helped both projects but predominantly gave Jaguar some credence in the Ford camp.

In November 1992 Jaguar set about the sourcing of parts to build the X-100 and found tremendous support from suppliers, despite the fact that there was no money on the table at this stage or, indeed, an agreement to produce the car. The very same month *Autocar* magazine published an 'exclusive' on the new Jaguar V8 sports car. Splashed across its front cover was a very credible artist's impression of the car, although the inside pictures owed more to the stillborn F-type than the X-100. In their editorial, headed 'The F-type lives', they demonstrated first-hand knowledge of what had happened that year, even down to Jaguar's thoughts about using a modified version of the existing XJ-S suspension. However, the impression was given that Ford had now backed the project officially. Their closing statement said a lot: 'For the lovers of Jaguar sports cars, the next three and a half years (until the launch of X-100) are going to seem interminable'!

To summarise, once the design strategy had been conceived and the concepts prepared, the sequence of events that accompanied the hectic birth of the X-100 project in 1992 was as follows:

- March – Theme selection
- March/April – Feasibility review
- June – Market research
- June/July – Post-research design changes
- June/July – Review and agreement on one design
- July – Review clinic in the USA
- August – Post-US review design changes
- September – Feasibility review
- September – Overall review

1993: moving forward

And so into 1993, only the second year of the X-100 design programme, with Jaguar working – unofficially – towards a launch date of 1996. The first move came in February, when a fibreglass representation of the car was shown to the US dealer network, where it was met with great acclaim, although they wanted changes like more chrome and good old-fashioned wire wheels. This provided positive feedback for the Jaguar team and must have sown the seed of Ford eventually giving the project its final approval – but not yet! Ford still considered that 80 per cent of the Jaguar business depended on saloons, so it was difficult to justify major expenditure on a new Jaguar sports car.

In March 1993 the options were still open-ended and varied. Jaguar could carry out yet another upgrade to the existing XJS design (which, of course, happened anyway); they could fit their forthcoming new engine (the AJ-26) into the XJS bodyshell with or without further design upgrades; or they could continue with development of the X-100, but only as a convertible (to save money) though making it available with a fitted hardtop.

Back in the UK, Jaguar remained convinced of the potential of the X-100, and work had to get under way quickly on the many aspects of the car. Firstly, and right from the outset, the X-100 would have to use the existing XJS floorpan (which dated right back to 1968 and the first XJ6). This requirement was set in stone, as the floorpan is arguably the most expensive item to engineer; there wasn't the money or time to develop a new base for the car, so the good old XJS would be recycled for this purpose.

With this firmly in mind the next consideration was the existing suspension layout. A famous bit of Jaguar engineering – the independent rear suspension, that dated back to 1961 and the E-type, and had served the company admirably – was considered, to save money. The same also applied to the front suspension, as both would easily fit onto the existing floorpan. The rear package was not considered a viable option, however. Suspension technology had moved on, and at this time the XJS still had inboard rear disc brakes (more costly to service), although this was soon to change. The next choice was to adapt the floorpan to accept the newer, more practical and economical alternative, the X-300 saloon rear suspension, itself based on the XJ40.

The front suspension also caused problems, since the XJS fitment couldn't be achieved given that the X-100 would be powered by the new AJ26 V8 engine, which was smaller, lighter, and would sit further forward in the car. The main oil sump was also situated at the front of the new engine (not at the rear as with the Jaguar V12 and AJ6 engines), so it would foul the existing XJS subframe. Height restrictions under the sloping bonnet of the X-100 also affected engine mounting, and here too the technology had moved on, which would mean unreasonable changes to the existing set-up. Lastly, the existing XJS subframe was not known for its longevity and this too had to be addressed in the new car.

Jaguar's thoughts therefore turned to using the subframe developed for the X-300, but again space was a problem so initially a steel subframe was designed before worries about fatigue ruled this out. Eventually new technology came into play, with an intriguing light and stiff alloy design being adopted which would be unique to the X-100.

As for the bodywork, Jaguar had learnt a lot from Ford with their new Mustang design, and the 'no adjust' body-build principle was adopted, so that instead of car bodies being designed and built with adjustable hinges and tolerances to allow for manual adjustment on the assembly line, tighter tolerances and better build quality enabled each panel or door to fit first time. This eliminated the need for the hand-fitting of panels during assembly, and the expensive and time-consuming use of lead loading, shimming, etc, all of which made the car easier and cheaper to build.

Conceived back in the 1960s, the XJS floorpan – indeed, the car – was always a heavy structure, so it was necessary to lighten everything where possible. For example, a lot of the old style strengthening was removed in favour of panel upgrades with smaller, higher stressed reinforcements. There would also be a 60 per cent reduction in the welding required on the car's bodyshell, as the number of panels required to build an X-100 were 30 per cent less than in an XJS.

All the tooling work for the X-100 body was given to the Japanese Ogihara company, well known for their expertise and quality and already working on the Ford Mustang project. They also worked closely with Jaguar to set up the body-in-white assembly facility at the Castle Bromwich factory in Birmingham.

A new car, a new engine and new transmission

As already mentioned, it was always intended that the new car would take the latest AJ26 Jaguar V8 engine, under development at the time. The AJ26 was only the fourth completely new engine totally designed and built by Jaguar. The first, the well-known XK six-cylinder engine, had powered all Jaguar models from 1948 until 1971 and remained in use in a substantial number of cars even thereafter; then had come the legendary V12 unit used from 1971 through to 1997; and most recently there had been the AJ-6 (later AJ-16) multi-valve straight six, built from 1983 to 1997, which replaced the XK unit. Jaguar's problem was that a new engine was vital to reduce the overall weight of the car, to improve efficiency and to retain refinement. Jaguar's

V12 engine was costly to build and wouldn't pass updated US emissions controls in place since 1995, and the six-cylinder engine was not refined or efficient enough and was too heavy.

The new V8 represented a major step forward in technology and performance terms, for which Jaguar had started with a clean sheet of paper in the late 1980s. Surveying the needs and perceptions of their market, it was decided that the most vital requirements were good performance with refinement, a high standard of durability and quality, and reasonable cost of ownership and maintenance. As well as these idyllic objectives Jaguar also had to consider ever more stringent legislation worldwide on emissions, fuel consumption, CO_2 and even noise pollution. Safety issues were also a factor, since a neat compact engine provided the designers with the optimum amount of space to protect occupants from front-end collisions.

The tradition of utilising six cylinders was soon abandoned for reasons of refinement and possible problems with hydrocarbon emissions. Ten cylinders would have created inherent imbalance problems for such a refined car, and 12 cylinders were immediately vetoed on a cost basis. Nevertheless, it was recognised that a V formation would make for a compact unit, and would be very acceptable in the valued US market. The solution, therefore, was to use eight cylinders, which offered a good weight saving and, ultimately, excellent engine refinement.

The concept of a V8 engine had been mooted by Jaguar earlier, even before the Ford take-over, but this time round it was a serious contender from the outset. It was considered vital that the refinement of the finished product should be at least as good as the then current Jaguar V12 power unit, and, indeed, competition was particularly stiff from the likes of Lexus, who in 1990 had launched their own superbly designed, refined and economical V8 engine for their top-of-the-range LS400 saloon. It was considered equally vital that a Jaguar like the X-100, a prestigious sporting car, should have a bespoke Jaguar engine, despite the fact that Ford had been developing their own V8 Romeo unit. This was a lesson that Jaguar had learnt earlier, when British Leyland had tried to influence their engine installations.

Early AJ26 engine under test. (JDHT)

Development of the new AJ26 engine (which later, just prior to the launch of the X-100, was renamed the AJ-V8) was carried out at Jaguar's ex-Daimler factory in Radford, Coventry, where Jaguar engines and axles were manufactured and assembled. Though the development work was Jaguar's they had the assistance of Ford personnel and their considerable experience with V8 engines.

Radford was a very old plant, built in 1912 specifically for vehicle production, and serious consideration was given to producing the new V8 engine there. Another possibility was that Jaguar might build a new facility to produce the V8, but neither of these schemes was financially viable at the time. Ford already had their fairly new and technologically advanced facility in Bridgend in Wales, which had spare capacity and the necessary expertise to produce the Jaguar engines economically and efficiently. The hard but necessary decision was therefore taken to move engine production away from Coventry. This would ultimately lead to the closure of the old Daimler factory in 1996, around the same time as the X-100 was launched.

Publicly, the first details of the new V8 engine to be produced at Bridgend came in *Autocar* magazine in Mach 1993, along with revealing spy pictures of the then still under development X-300 saloon. Even at that stage *Autocar* suspected that the new engine would make its first appearance in the X-100 sports car project, but reckoned that it would only be pushing out about 260bhp, well under the final figure.

It took only 12 months from the official go-ahead to production of the first prototype V8 engine, and very little changed after that point apart from interesting and weight-saving features such as the replacement of conventional intake manifolds by Polyamide plastic composite with integrated fuel rails, which also provided good external thermal insulation and a nice, aesthetically smooth finish to the top of the engine. Further details of the AJ-V8's technological advances will be covered in the next chapter.

The XJS and even the XJ40 saloon proved ideal test beds to try out the new engine, and at one time even Directors of the company were running around in drone cars equipped thus, no one who saw them being any the wiser that under the bonnet there lurked something entirely new.

In total £160 million was spent on the development of the AJ-V8, including the setting up of production facilities at Bridgend and all the tooling. This amounted to just short of the budget provided by Ford. Not only was the new engine delivered on time and within its financial parameters, but it was also a foot shorter than the old six-cylinder engine and 90lb lighter than the AJ-16, which permitted greater freedom when it came to designing the rest of the car. Because the engine was on target, it was decided that its launch should coincide with that of the new car.

To accompany the engine, a highly efficient cooling system was patented by Jaguar for the X-100, with low volume capacity which permitted the engine to warm up in less than four minutes, reducing engine wear and providing a more comfortable environment for the occupants in cold weather.

The new engine also got a new gearbox. Following the poor sales response to the earlier XJSs, proved later with the X-300 saloons, it was decided that the X-100 would only be available as an automatic. The work of developing the new transmission was entrusted to the German ZF company, and although the gearbox chosen was also to be used by other manufacturers Jaguar were significantly involved in its development, to ensure that it suited the X-100's specification (and those of subsequent models), so joint patents were taken out by the two companies. This was to be Jaguar's first five-speed automatic transmission, and featured the tried and tested J-gate operation first seen on the XJ40 back in 1986. The result was the fully electronic ZF 5HP 24 gearbox, specially designed for mating to V8 engines. The X-100 was to be the first Jaguar car ever equipped with a fully electronic 'box. There are more details on this too in the next chapter.

A surprise announcement came in June of 1993 from Tom Walkinshaw of JaguarSport (already committed to building the Aston Martin DB7 at Bloxham after the demise of the Jaguar XJ220), who declared his intention to produce a two-seater Jaguar to rival the E-type, costing around £30,000. It would be a real drivers' car and up to 5,000 would be produced each year. Speculation followed that this would be released in 1996, coinciding with Jaguar's own X-100, but nothing actually came of the project – unless it turned out to be the later joint venture between Walkinshaw and Volvo to produce their stylish two-door coupé.

Financial support and final approval

It was now June 1993, and there had still been no formal approval of funds to build the X-100, even though Bob Dover and his team were getting to grips with the project. By this time it had come down to Ford and Jaguar seeking a commitment from the British Government of cash to assist the project – after all, Nissan had got significant support from the Government, so why not Jaguar? But only a month later the Government gave the thumbs down to financial support, and there were strong fears at Jaguar that the X-100 would finally be cancelled. Ford also insisted on more 'clinics', using the fibreglass cars to get better feedback and evaluation on the project's viability. Fortunately the support and interest expressed at these meetings surprised even Ford.

Whilst all this was happening Jaguar's Browns Lane Assembly Plant in Coventry was closing for its summer holiday, during which time the tracks were dismantled and over £50 million was invested in new assembly technology – all, at this time, to support production of the still to be announced X-300 saloon, but which would inevitably be used for the building of other Jaguar models too, not least, it was hoped, the new sports car. However, thoughts turned to the possibility of building the new Jaguar in Portugal, whose own government had offered £23 million of financial

Early camouflaging attempts designed to keep prying eyes at bay, although a lot of the initial work was done using XJSs. (JDHT)

support. This offer provided Jaguar with a gauntlet to be thrown at the feet of the British Government in the hope that it would reconsider its position. In the meantime, the first proper prototype was completed in September using the XJS floorpan, the AJ-V8 engine, and a representation of the X-100 bodywork, which was used for high-speed testing.

By the end of the year things were really hotting up, because the British *Car* magazine had printed spy photographs of the new car taken in Jaguar's own styling studio – something Jaguar had been trying hard to avoid. Even more importantly, on 1 December the UK Government announced a grant of £9.4 million plus additional support for the project. This effectively ruled out the Portuguese offer and forced Ford to also commit themselves in mid-December to £10 million of support for the X-100 programme, although even then only on the basis that commitment would not be given to any specific country for final production.

1994: X-100 is a goer

By February 1994 over 30 prototypes had been produced – most of them still substantially based on drone XJSs – for all sorts of test requirements, including hot and cold weather evaluation. Ogihara had also delivered the first 30 body-in-white shells. Even more importantly, by May Jaguar had produced two very significant prototypes (a Coupé and a Convertible) of the actual X-100, based on prototype tooling. These looked like the real thing, drove, and were substantially used as feasibility studies for production. The X-100 may have been based on the XJS floorpan, but in so many other ways it was technically very advanced. Multi-plexing the wiring saved something like two hours in assembling the electrics. A reduced number of sub-assemblies was also used, many of them assembled by outside suppliers to be delivered to the 'track' as required, which cut down overall production time. Parts were sourced from the best of Ford's suppliers around the world to ensure a class-leading final product.

For the Convertible model, the work of development was again given to Karmann, who had been responsible for the XJS Convertible. Initially there were thoughts of adopting a metal frame like that used by Mercedes, but this was abandoned in favour of the lighter and cheaper approach of a conventional fabric tonneau cover. Karmann's work on the X-100 resulted in a 10 per cent lighter frame construction than that used on the XJS, yet it was torsionally stiffer.

1994 was a busy year all round for Jaguar, as it saw the launch of the X-300 saloon and the final demise of

NEAR MISS

The Japanese company Ogihara, which had designed and built the body tooling for the X-100, suffered damage from a major earthquake in Kobe, where their factory was based. Had it not been for the fact that the Jaguar tooling had just left Japan en route to the UK, the subsequent loss would have set the XK8 launch back some considerable time.

the XJ40, and thoughts were well advanced towards running-down XJS production in view of the progress made on X-100. In September the evaluation programme of prototypes was well under way, and a month later the schedule for production tooling was agreed. This included final approval to suppliers who manufactured the various components, one of which was the dashboard moulding and instrument packs produced in-house by Ford at Enfield in Middlesex.

It is interesting to compare the development of X-100 alongside the then entirely new DB7 produced by Aston Martin, another Ford-owned company. After

Later camouflage. This car, a Convertible, looks more like the proverbial bread van, but it was all necessary to keep media eyes away. (JDHT)

the Ford take-over of Jaguar (and Aston Martin), Tom Walkinshaw – who had worked closely with Jaguar since the early 1980s on the XJS Touring Car Championship, the JaguarSport modified cars and, of course, the XJ220 – constructed a new prototype, code named Project XX. Using the XJ41 base body style, XJS underpinnings, and a supercharged version of the Jaguar AJ16 engine, the running prototype was abandoned by Jaguar but taken up by Aston, and although the DB7 turned out a very different animal to Project XX, the connections were very valid. By 1994 production of the Aston Martin DB7 was already well under way at the old Bloxham JaguarSport factory in Oxfordshire. Priced at nearly £80,000, the new Aston was on the road and had been exceptionally well received. Inevitably there was to be a lot of cross-over in the development of the DB7 and X-100, but how would Jaguar's new sports car compete with Aston Martin's? We had to wait another two years to find out!

1995: a hectic year of testing

With only 5,000 XJSs produced in 1995 the desperate need for the X-100 was confirmed. With development cars now undergoing even more intensive testing, X-100-clad examples received a rather Heath-

Robinson, yet effective, rubberised and moulded disguise to protect the final style from prying eyes. A fair number of these cars were subjected to extensive hot and cold climate testing in order to evaluate them fully, mostly on continuous eight-hour driving shifts. With and without cladding they were also subjected to continuous high-speed assessment at the Nardo circuit in Italy. Racing driver (and Ford consultant) Jackie Stewart was also involved in testing the X-100. During this period production tooling for 1,700 parts was established for the new model, although additional components were selected directly from the then-current Jaguar parts bin. Apart from the obvious XJS connection in the floorpan, a modified version of its seat frames was also utilised, which to some extent limited the development of new seats. Apparently no less than 22 different styles of seat were tried before arriving at the end result. Other parts came from and/or were modified from the X-300 saloons. These included the Teves braking system, the J-gate gear-select, the air conditioning system, upper steering column, door hinge assemblies, and even more mundane items like some of the switch-gear and the centre console arm-rest lid.

With more work carried out on the suspension, one of the advantages of utilising a new arrangement at the front was being able to accommodate anti-squat abilities, something the XJS didn't have. Also, spring rates and pitch were altered, and the rear suspension/axle mounting frame was taken from the supercharged version of the X-300 for extra stiffness. Similar enhancements were carried out to the X-300 power-assisted steering system used on the X-100.

Between 6 and 8 March 1995 Jaguar arranged seminar launches at their Whitley Engineering facility to which the technical press were invited to review the AJ-V8 engine. These were followed in April and May by press visits to the Ford plant in Bridgend, already set up to manufacture the new engine. By mid-1995 all was going well, except for the publication by *Autocar* and *Car* magazines of spy pictures of the X-100 in reduced camouflage undergoing high-speed testing at Nardo.

In October 1995 the first Evaluation Prototype was produced, which led to no less than 32 being built to test the effective and efficient build of the new car. These were effectively fully production-tooled cars assembled from substantially production parts on a specially prepared miniature production line at Browns Lane.

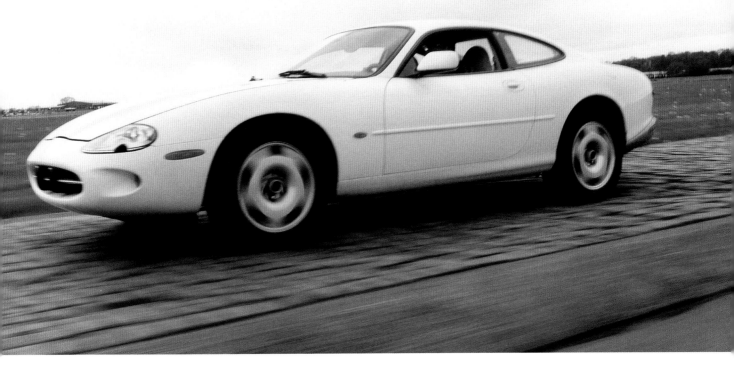

In August *Autocar* published a reasonably accurate artist's impression of the X-100, which was followed in October by six full pages of coverage, with *paparazzi* pictures of camouflaged cars and a sneak picture of an unclad car. A lot of detail was revealed in the accompanying article, where it was speculated that a six-speed manual gearbox version would also be made available.

1996: the final goal in sight

It was as late as February 1996 that the final software approval was given to ZF for the new five-speed gearbox. Moving on from this the next phase was to use some of the 30 fully functional X-100 prototypes for final testing, then for advertising and other photographic work. It was also in February that the very first AJ-V8 engine left the production line at Bridgend, while production of the gearboxes began in March.

It was also at about this time that the new car's name was settled, X-100 having been merely its in-house development code. 'F-type' was out because of its association with the previous ill-fated XJ41 project. 'XK', however, echoed past Jaguar successes in the sports car market, but XKF was felt to be too close to

An evaluation prototype being put through its paces at the Mira test track in Warwickshire. (JDHT)

the MGF model insignia. 'XK160' sounded good and continued the naming style used on the 1950s XKs, but it was felt to be just too retro for a significantly new car. XK8 therefore prevailed in the end, and perhaps quite rightly so.

The media hype was building up as, in January of that year, *Autocar* produced supposedly undercover details of 100 secret cars due out in 1996, amongst which was, of course, the XK8. They targeted the car as 'the biggest launch of the year'. Less than a month later the same magazine provided more news on the XK8, declaring that it would be publicly launched at the Geneva Motor Show that March. Interestingly, at the same time they claimed to have knowledge that a supercharged version would become available, to be called the XKR8!

A small upset for Jaguar came in March, when *The Times* newspaper printed a report that the new Jaguar V8 engine was merely a re-vamped Ford unit from the US. Although Ford under-wrote the whole Jaguar engine project, apparently only two parts came from their parts bin – a woodruff key and the sump plug.

One of the first batch of true production cars, still under test at this stage. (JDHT)

Whether that was Jaguar marketing coming into play or not, the fact is that the new AJ26 engine was designed by Jaguar.

At the International Geneva Motor Show that month, Jaguar did indeed pre-launch the new car, now publicly known as the XK8. But the engine compartment was not revealed, nor were any specific details of the car announced. It was purely a pre-launch 'showcase' for the new model, meant to echo that of the E-type back in 1961. It was also in March that engine production started at Bridgend, while construction of the transmissions commenced in April.

April also saw the production of another completed 100 cars. Effectively these could have been sold to the public, but 50 were used for in-house management evaluation of how they would cope with normal everyday use.

The first batch of true production cars was made in June, with the first (Job 1) leaving the line on the 4th of that month. Of this first run of 170 cars, 20 were taken for further management evaluation while the rest formed part of the stock build-up ready for the official launch in October.

It was also in June that the new AJ-V8 engine was publicly launched, and soon afterwards the specification details of the new car were announced. A lot of pre-launch selling took place during the summer, whilst production got up to speed. In overall terms, while the XJS could only be built at the rate of 110 cars per week, up to 250 of the more efficently made XK8 could be built in the same time, the new car needing only 150 operatives to assemble it and being 30 per cent quicker to build. It also proved to be 'best in class' when it came to the integrity of fitment of the component parts from the many suppliers used. By August the Jaguar Browns Lane factory had produced no less than 2,000 XK8s ready for despatch to the dealers, with production being geared at this stage to a ratio of three Convertibles to two Coupés.

Summary

Through good planning and management, early parts sourcing and a great deal of faith from all involved, the XK8 had been delivered in just 30 months from programme approval. Around 80 per cent of its parts were entirely new, with only 10 per cent carried over from the XJ Series saloons. Though it took 30 per cent less body panels to construct the XK8 shell than the XJS, build quality was dramatically improved and torsional stiffness was increased by 25 per cent. Add a new engine, new gearbox, and new axles and suspension, and there you have it: the XK8.

Job 1 – the very first production XK8 off the Browns Lane line in 1996. (JDHT)

The XK8 had arrived. These are very early Coupé and Convertible production models in Jaguar's styling 'garden' at Whitley, with (on the left) Styling Director Geoff Lawson and Fergus Pollock. (JDHT)

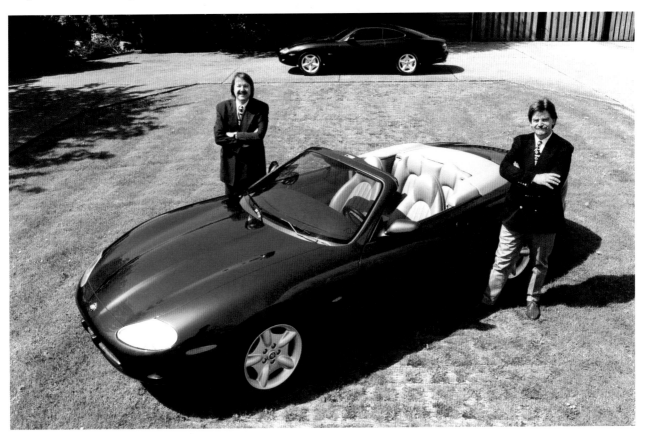

Chapter Two

The new car in detail

The heart of any car is its engine and Jaguar had, up to this time, only produced three basic engine designs: firstly the legendary XK straight six, launched in 1948 in its XK120 sports, the engine that powered every single production Jaguar until 1971 and continued in production until 1992; then the awesome V12 that powered the E-type Series 3 sports from 1971 and stayed in production for top-of-the-range saloons until 1997; and lastly the AJ6/AJ16 multi-valve straight six introduced in 1983 for the XJ-S, which powered the majority of production Jaguars until the introduction of

the AJ26. It appeared to be Jaguar policy to launch a new engine in a sporting model first, and history repeated itself when the new AJ26 (from here on the AJ-V8) was introduced in the XK8.

The basic advantages of the new engine were that it was shorter and lighter, both of which had numerous advantages. Pro rata it was more powerful, refined, quiet, and frugal than previous Jaguar six-cylinder engines and was more economical and as quiet and refined as the V12.

The engine is of four-cam design with a 90° V formation, apparently to minimise any out-of-balance problems normally associated with V8 engines. Of square cylinder dimensions (86mm bore and stroke),

The AJ-V8 installation in the early XK8. This car has standard (non CATS) suspension. (Nigel Thorley)

the cubic capacity is 3,996cc, which Jaguar claimed provided the best compromise between the conflicts of power, torque, economy, emissions and vibration levels. Rated at 290bhp at 6,100rpm, 80 per cent of the maximum torque is available throughout a range of 1,400 to 6,400rpm.

It is interesting to compare the performance of the early V8 engine to the outgoing Jaguar power units of the time:

	Cubic Capacity	bhp	@rpm	bhp output per litre	Maximum torque
AJ-V8	3,996cc	290	6,100	72.6	290lb ft @4,250rpm
AJ16	3,980cc	249	4,800	61.0	289lb ft @4,000rpm
V12	5,993cc	318	5,350	52.0	353lb ft @2,850rpm

Jaguar claimed at the time the highest specific output of any engine in this class and the highest torque per litre in class at peak torque and high engine speeds:

AJ-V8 contemporary comparisons with the opposition

	Cubic capacity	bhp	Maximum torque
AJ-V8	3,996cc	290	290lb ft
BMW 804	3,982cc	282	310lb ft
Mercedes 320	3,199cc	228	200lb ft
Porsche 911 Carrera	3,600cc	285	251lb ft

The engine block was cleverly designed to be lightweight yet to provide significant stiffness and torsional strength from its cast ribbed-web connected banks and closed deck design. Further, in order to save weight there were no conventional iron liners to the cylinder bores, which were instead lined with nickel silicon carbide (Nikasil) to a thickness of 0.08mm, saving 15lb in weight and providing supposedly high wear-resistance because its ultra-smooth surface minimises friction. Developed for Formula One, this new technology – also adopted by other manufacturers such as BMW – meant installing a new plating plant and an all-new low pressure alloy die-casting process to ensure low porosity.

Cosworth produced the unique twin cylinder heads for Jaguar. Heavily ribbed, these provide stiffness, minimise radiated noise and are each a mirror image of the other. An 18mm offset makes for compact head design and bulk and the unusually long cylinder head bolts ensure an excellent head-to-block seal. The five-bearing crankshaft is made from spheroidal graphite cast iron, while the conrods are forged by the highly accurate Krebsoge powder sintering technique. Alloy flat top, short skirt, low friction pistons are used.

The new engine incorporated variable cam phasing on the inlet cams, with a 30° range of adjustment which not only helped performance but also contributed towards low emission levels.

A four valves per cylinder configuration was adopted but with more slender diameter shafts, operated by low-mass aluminium bucket tappets. Given this conventional set-up, Jaguar opted for larger valves in proportion to port size than their competitors' engines, to enhance performance. Another weight reduction came about by drilling the chilled cast iron camshafts from end to end, saving around 1lb per cam. Cam drive is by four single-row chains rather than a toothed belt, which was more common practice then as now. Chains were adopted to minimise the depth of the engine and also provided greater engine safety in service.

A 28° angle between the inlet and exhaust valves facilitates a narrow, squish-free pent-roof combustion chamber, minimising heat loss and providing for high tolerances to exhaust gas recirculation and thereby improving emissions further. A very high 10.75:1 compression ratio was chosen. Yet another benefit to emissions was gained by fitting close-coupled catalytic

General layout of the AJ-V8 engine heads, manifolds and cylinder block. (Nigel Thorley collection)

Unique attributes of the air intake system on the V8 engine. (Nigel Thorley collection)

Patented by Jaguar, the split coolant flow from the water pump provides best-in-class efficiency. (Nigel Thorley collection)

converters and thin-wall exhaust manifolds, while a very fast from-cold engine warm-up is assured by a unique (for the time) low volume 'split block' cooling system (see below).

Plastics were used extensively, not only to save weight. The intake manifolds were moulded from Polyamide composite, which is both lightweight and has the added advantage of providing external thermal insulation and an attractive smooth finish to conventional castings. This also enabled Jaguar to accommodate an integrated fuel rail into the manifold to reduce complexity and improve injector targeting.

A new Nippondenso 32-bit electronic engine management system was adopted for the AJ-V8 engine and proved to be the best in its class. Optimising adjustment of the throttle openings, it facilitated better idle speed control and cruise control, and offered improved drivability and exhaust emissions control.

Jaguar made great play of the fast warm-up time for the AJ-V8 (less than four minutes from cold), and the Society of Automotive Engineers gave them an award for the XK8's cooling system. Using a split system, the water pump delivers water separately, with 50 per cent of the coolant delivered into a gallery bypassing the bores, delivering the flow to the cylinder heads at the rear of the engine, and then mixing with the remaining 50 per cent of coolant used to cool the bores. Jaguar also claimed that the high velocity of coolant delivery prevented localised boiling with less than 2° difference in metal temperature between the front and rear of the engine.

Manufacture of the first engines for production cars got under way in May 1996 and had built up to 35 units a day within a month.

Transferring the power

A new car and a new engine deserved a new transmission, but due to the unpopularity of 'stick shift' models for many years Jaguar opted not to offer a manual gearbox. Instead, ZF provided Jaguar's first five-speed automatic gearbox, the ZF 5HP 24 utilising advanced micro-processor control.

Using a 32-bit intelligent electronic system, the gearbox optimised gearshift points according to driver, conditions, and even temperature. The low inertia torque converter design allowed for the fitment of an advanced slip-controlled clutch, to improve fuel economy and the refinement of gear changes. The established J-gate operation, first seen in the XJ40 saloon, was retained for XK8 models.

Billed as a 'fill for life' sealed unit, the gearbox theoretically required no maintenance during the life of the car, but information supplied later in this publication will verify that service maintenance is highly recommended!

At the wheels

Jaguar adopted the ZF Servotronic speed sensitive rack-and-pinion steering system for the XK8, but with a special variable ratio feature to benefit low-speed manoeuvring and high-speed stability and to provide

The new ZF 5HP 24 five-speed automatic transmission adopted for the XK8. (Nigel Thorley collection)

positive centre feel at the steering wheel. The system allows for power assistance to be speed-proportioned, while the positive centre feel provides stability when travelling in a straight line and in crosswinds, but at the same time doesn't increase parking effort. The variable

General layout of the drivetrain of the normally aspirated early XK8. (Nigel Thorley collection)

Jaguar's combined wishbone with coil spring and telescopic shock absorber design for the XK8. (Nigel Thorley collection)

ratio reduces the number of steering wheel turns for parking and also reduces excessive response to driver input at high speed.

For the front suspension Jaguar opted to use a proven design but with a new departure. A double, unequal length wishbone design combined with coil springs and telescopic shock absorbers is an established concept, but in the XK8 the road springs are mounted directly to the body to improve handling and durability and to reduce suspension bush loads. Spring rates were developed to create less stress, and the hydraulic mounts (hydramounts, which are filled with oil) between the front cross-member and engine are tuned to ensure spring loads remain isolated.

The all-alloy front crossbeam identified in the last chapter, designed to aircraft quality standards, weighs in at only 15.8kg and is treated with Dacromet to guard against corrosion in contact with steel components.

As previously mentioned, the rear suspension owes a lot to the then-current X-300 (XJR) saloon design. It is made up of an A-frame and monostrut design using a pendulum arrangement to allow fore and aft movement of the rear wheels at the inner fulcrums to enhance ride comfort. It also provides for good axle location.

An extra-cost option, initially only for Coupé models,

was the unique Jaguar 'CATS' (Computer Active Technology Suspension) system. This optimises the ride and handling according to conditions by means of uprated springs to increase the roll stiffness and adaptive dampers under electronic control. Sensors at the front and rear monitor the road and handling conditions and alter the electronic dampers to stiffen or soften settings accordingly. At start-up the dampers default to a firm setting, but once on the move above 5mph they revert to a softer setting. The settings continue to alter in micro-seconds when cornering, braking or on poor road surfaces.

The XK8's brakes were vastly uprated from those used on the old XJS. For example, larger ventilated discs (28mm x 305mm) are used at both the front and rear. Still using the Teves ABS system, improvements for the XK8 included the fitment of Automatic Stability Control (ASC). If a wheel starts to spin under power, the ABS control module uses the information to calculate the amount of torque reduction (eg engine power) required to eliminate the spin. Another additional aspect taken from the ABS system is Traction Control, which acts in conjunction with the Stability Control to reduce wheelspin in slippery conditions.

Wheels chosen for the XK8 at launch were the five-spoke (later known as Revolver) 8J x 17in alloy fitted with Pirelli P-Zero 245/50 ZR 17 tyres. These tyres had an asymmetric tread pattern with the outside tread area providing the best grip and the inside grooves providing good drainage. Chromium-plated versions of the five-spoke wheels were also available as an extra-cost option.

A further extra-cost option was the fitment of 8J x 18in (9J at the rear) seven-spoke (Flute) alloys, with Pirelli P-Zero 245/45 ZR 18 tyres at the front and 255/45 at the rear, the first time a production Jaguar had ever been equipped with different sized wheels and tyres front to back. The front tyres were unidirectional (different left to right), so are not interchangeable, while the rear tyres were asymmetric. These larger wheels and tyres were an integral part of the CATS suspension package on the Coupé but were also available to Convertible owners at the time. Normally a space saver spare wheel was provided in the boot area for all markets except the US.

Security and safety aspects

Security has become an important issue on cars over the last few years, so the XK8 had to accommodate the latest state-of-the-art technology if it was to be a successful seller. Taking a lead from the then-current XJ

The Sport interior of an early XK8 with cloth seat inserts, rare to find today. (Nigel Thorley collection)

saloons, a remote-controlled key fob transmitter, operated by radio frequency, controls the locking and unlocking of the vehicle. For extra security it uses a rolling code, which changes every time the unit is operated, with over four billion combinations. The key fob controls the locking and alarm process, headlamp operation, and the electric boot lid mechanism.

Internal security was monitored by sensors. A sophisticated glass-break sensor can detect the sound of breaking glass and set the alarm off, while perimeter sensing protects the car from forced entry through the doors, bonnet and boot. It is also possible to programme the security alarm system to activate automatically if the car is left with all the doors and windows closed and the ignition key removed.

All XK8s are fitted with a supplementary restraint system involving twin full-sized airbags activated by an ECU responding to electromechanical sensing. One airbag is situated within the steering wheel centre boss and the other behind the wood-veneered facia panel on the passenger side.

Interior features

Using traditional Jaguar features of wood and leather, the interior of the early XK8s allowed two choices of finish, although the layout and controls remained the same for both. These were the Sport (or standard) trim and the Classic.

According to Jaguar at the time, the Sport was considered a more modern approach to trim finish, geared to the younger, sportier buyer – an idea poached from other marques. The seat facings were covered in a

The Sport interior as most were bought, with leather seat centre panels with distinctive horizontal pleating. Note the high-contrast trim colours used and the dark-stained maple woodwork, all standard features of the Sport interior. (Nigel Thorley)

This picture shows two elements of the XK8 – the unique seat style of the Sport model, and the inadequate legroom for rear seat passengers. (Nigel Thorley)

Subtle trim colours, walnut veneer and different seating style differentiate the Classic (below) from the Sport trim option. (Nigel Thorley)

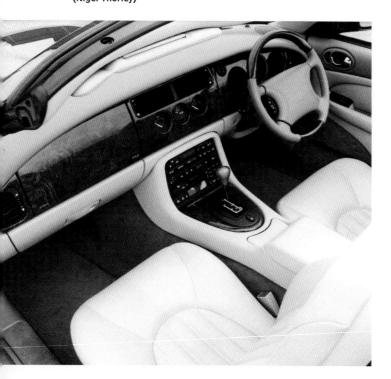

combination of leather with cloth centre panels, the seats having three horizontal flutes with charcoal stitching. Trim colours were either charcoal or oatmeal. The conventional four-spoke steering wheel, along with the gear knob, were trimmed in partly perforated charcoal leather to complement the black carpet throughout. The black facia top panel was co-ordinated with dark grey stained maple veneer. As an extra-cost option the purchaser could also opt for full leather seating, with horizontal flutes in charcoal, oatmeal or cream finish.

The Sport trim was not offered in the North American market and was to represent a very small percentage of sales everywhere except in the UK, where Jaguar anticipated a 60 per cent take-up.

The Classic option was decidedly more traditional Jaguar, fairly and squarely aimed at existing Jaguar buyers and those who preferred luxury and prestige. The seats were leather and featured five vertical flutes with colour-keyed stitching. A burr walnut veneer was used for the main facia area, centre console and door mounted switch-packs, accompanied by a half wood/leather steering wheel and wood grain gear knob. Seating, facia, door trims and carpets were all colour co-ordinated.

The instrument pack used on the XK8 was new at the time and was later adopted for the V8-engined XJ saloons. The main speedometer, rev counter and fuel/water temperature gauges were in front of the driver, while the analogue clock and auxiliary gauges for oil pressure and the battery were mounted centrally. The deeply in-set gauges in front of the driver were continuously illuminated and remained clearly visible even when driving in a tunnel without the exterior lights on. A development of Jaguar's on-board computer and message centre was used, and the centre console took its lead from XJ saloons of the period, and with a quieter and more efficient air conditioning system as standard equipment than was previously used on the XJS.

All models were supplied with an 80 watt audio system as standard. This comprised multi-waveband stereo radio/cassette, four speakers (one in each door and rear quarter casings), and a power-operated rear wing mounted aerial. Alternatively, at extra cost a Harman/Kardon Premium sound system could be specified, producing 240 watts, with eight-channel power amplifier and a nine (Coupé) or ten (Convertible) speaker layout. A six-disc CD auto-changer could also be specified on all models.

External attributes

Jaguar had been very clever in incorporating styling cues from previous models like the XJ220 and E-type, yet had kept the car very up-to-date in its appeal. The Coupé was undoubtedly the prettiest of the two styles, but the Convertible (nearly always a compromise) had a virtually unique styling flow for the period.

Contrary to prevailing practice in some prestige convertibles, Jaguar opted not to go for a fully retracting hood arrangement with an integrated metal tonneau cover. Instead, there was a good old studded leather tonneau, which had to be fitted manually. Cost played a part in this decision, but it also meant that space for the fuel tank and the all-important luggage accommodation in the boot wasn't compromised. At the XK8's launch, Jaguar commented that the hood standing proud with a prominent cover epitomised the English sporting car – good try, Jaguar!

Trying to design a stylish and aerodynamic sports car must always have its compromises if it is to be both practical and road legal. Jaguar had to make such a compromise at the front, for instance, with the fitment of the legally required (in the UK anyway) number plate. But other aspects of the XK8's style were characterised by clean, flowing lines. Its mix of traditionalism and good modern design is epitomised by the specially designed headlamp units, comprising a neutral lens for turn signals, a very small side light, a projection lens for dipped headlamp beam, and an ellipsoid reflector for the main beam, all encapsulated into a single unit which, in the better specified models, also included a retractable washer jet behind an extendable chromed fillet.

There was a surprising lack of chrome finish to the exterior of the early XK8s, although cars intended for the North American market were supplied with chromed door mirror backs and door handles.

What price success?

Retail selling prices for the XK8 at launch in September 1996 were:

XK8 Coupé	£47,950	$64,900
XK8 Convertible	£54,950	$72,455

These prices were for the 'base' models, so didn't include such items as Classic trim, 18in wheels, cruise control, or even a CD player. To fully spec an XK8 at this time would have set you back more than £8,000 extra.

Side on – a direct comparison between the Convertible and Coupé models, both of which are aesthetically pleasing and contemporary. Both are early models with the optional Flute wheels. (Nigel Thorley)

Full specifications of the original models will be found at the back of this book.

TOP AWARD

Coinciding with the launch of the XK8, Jaguar Cars was voted 'Britain's Top Manufacturer' in the Manufacturing Industry Achievement Awards. Sponsored by *The Engineer*, the award recognised the major quality, productivity and management improvements made at Jaguar, specifically citing the work done on the XK8.

Full frontal – the XK8 displays classic proportions not that dissimilar to the 1960s E-type or 1990s XJ220. (Nigel Thorley)

The cat is back

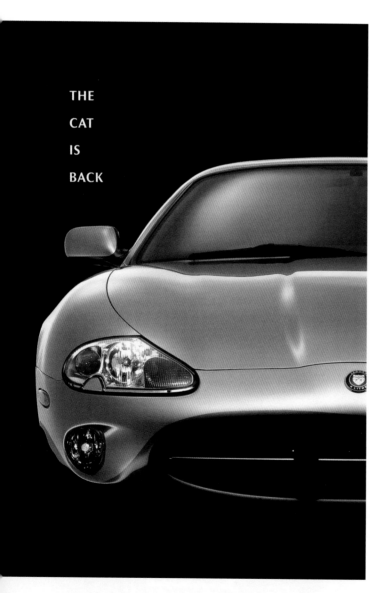

THE
CAT
IS
BACK

Jaguar's marketing slogan for the new car, 'The Cat is Back', was a good ploy to revitalise their sporting car image. (Nigel Thorley collection)

Thirty months from plan to production is all it took Jaguar to bring the XK8 to launch, a significant achievement. Now it was time for the marketing department and Jaguar's advertising agency, J. Walter Thompson, to get to grips with the new car.

Jaguar intended that the XK8 should appeal to a broader market than the out-going XJS, attracting both luxury and younger 'premium sports car' buyers, as the marketing men called them. To set the scene, the luxury sports car sector of the market only accounted for 55,000 car sales worldwide in 1995, with almost half of that market in North America, 25 per cent in Germany and a mere 8 per cent in the UK. The company therefore targeted a first full-year sales figure of 12,000 XK8s to be sold worldwide, of which 40 per cent would be Coupés and 60 per cent Convertibles. Of this total, 60 per cent would be earmarked for the US, of which 70 per cent would be Convertibles, reflecting the strong preference for the latter in the American market.

'THE HERITAGE OF GOOD DESIGN IS LIKE DNA'

'Our goal was to create a shape that communicates integrity and a sense of honesty. The finished design must express a "fitness for purpose" that bears a direct relationship to the mechanical components underneath. It's very easy to design a car that's a pastiche of cars, something that's trendy and hot. We worked very hard to avoid that temptation. Overall, we strove to bring obvious links with the past but without copying. The heritage of good design is like DNA, it must be traceable through history but not necessarily an exact duplicate.'

— Geoff Lawson,
Jaguar Director of Styling

The Geneva launch of the XK8 rekindled the razzamatazz of the 1960s E-type launch, with a wooden crate unveiling the car to an eager media. (Reprinted from *Autocar* magazine)

After achieving a peak of nearly 30 per cent of the market sales for this type of vehicle in the UK in 1988, Jaguar's share had taken a terrible knock due to the age of the XJS and increasing competition, particularly from Porsche, BMW and Mercedes. By contrast, in the US Jaguar had only ever achieved a total of 11.7 per cent of the market at best, and this fell considerably despite BMW being a minor player at the time, while even Porsche and Mercedes had been losing out to cars like the Lexus SC400.

Having said all this, a major market research project carried out by Jaguar identified that 81 per cent of XJS owners were completely satisfied with their cars. It also confirmed that loyalty to the brand was a major reason for buying, whereas Porsche owners were more likely to target performance as their reason to buy, while with Mercedes it was style and resale value. Another interesting revelation in this survey was that the majority of XJS owners tended to be older than the average for a prestige sporting vehicle, most likely retired or female.

Two key types of potential new customer were targeted for the XK8. Firstly, those who had rejected the XJS for quite rational reasons. Research revealed these to be people who were attracted emotionally to a Jaguar but who, despite Jaguar's improvements in build quality, hadn't perceived this due to the limited changes made to the XJS over the years. The somewhat radically new XK8 could address this issue, complemented by the three-year/60,000-mile mechanical warranty that reinforced Jaguar's commitment to quality.

The other key group were those who had previously rejected the image of Jaguar sporting models like the XJS. The style didn't fit their own image – they wanted something new, exciting, perhaps state-of-the-art, and here again Jaguar were confident that the new XK8 fitted that bill.

In an early statement from Jaguar's Sales and Marketing Training Manager to the dealers, he said: 'The new model will revitalise Jaguar's sports car range and rebuild the company's sports car presence in markets around the world. XK8 will compete in the luxury sports car market, primarily against the Mercedes SL, BMW 840 and Porsche 911. The target customer is likely to be male, aged about 42. This is younger than XJS and reflects the more youthful, sporty image of the XK8.'

Jaguar planned to 'drip-feed' information on the new car to the media and public over a period of seven months leading up to the British Motor Show in October, commencing at the beginning of March with

A LEAF FROM MG

The decision to 'drip-feed' the launch of the XK8 followed the successful pre-launch of the MGF at around the same time. It worked so well for MG-Rover that Jaguar adopted the same approach for their own new sports car.

the release of scant details and styling pictures to the media.

The XK8 Coupé had its first UK public airing at the Royal College of Art in London, where it was on display from 11 to 20 March as part of an exhibition celebrating the college's 100th anniversary. More importantly, however, the car soon afterwards had its first major public showing at the Geneva Motor Show. This was perfectly planned, as the E-type had been revealed to the public at the same show 35 years earlier. Following a similar 'launch' treatment to that of the E-type, the car – an Antigua Blue Coupé – revolved on a turntable, protected from early viewing by a wooden crate which was ceremoniously hoisted aloft to reveal the car in all its splendour.

It was certainly the star of the show in terms of interest and media hype, but apparently many questions were raised as to whether the car was 'right'. It was inevitably compared with the Aston Martin DB7, launched two years earlier and also based on the XJS floorpan, and there were comparisons with other cars too, not least the E-type. Was the XK8 too retro? Were the wheels too small for the body? Was the overhang too great at the rear? Was the cabin too cramped? Was the nose right? And so on. One difference to the E-type's launch in 1961 was that there were no XK8s to drive or be driven in, and the bonnet was locked tight so that no one could view the new V8 engine.

It wasn't until April that the Convertible got its first showing, this time at the New York Motor Show, again echoing the launch of the E-type roadster at this event back in 1961. Later the same month the Coupé and Convertible were shown together at the Turin Motor Show. All of these first showings were intended to do no more than whet people's appetites, but engine technical seminars were set up for the press on the basis that information would be embargoed until 4 June.

Then in June Jaguar finally released information on the AJ-V8 engine, so that by August the motoring press were publishing the full low-down on the new engine in their magazines and declaring themselves very impressed with the results. All they now wanted to do was drive a car to evaluate what Jaguar was telling them – that it was class-leading and superlative, even by Lexus standards. In late June and early July what seemed like an endless programme of dealer and distributor ride-and-drives took place around the world, to hype up the sales teams for the eventual public launch.

In August, by a stroke of luck, the United States Government announced it was phasing out a 10 per cent luxury car tax on cars that cost over $34,000. With the imminent launch of the XK8, this played into Jaguar's hands.

One of the very early production cars, in this case used by Bob Dover, taken on a trip to Cambridge about four months prior to the XK8's public launch. (Nigel Thorley)

The usual crop of press events now gave the journalists a chance to drive and assess the new cars in readiness for its public launch. The world dealer launch was held in Vancouver during the first week of September. Coinciding with this, around 50 XK8s were subjected to regular daily use by Jaguar managers and directors, being assessed for everything from daily commuting to long-distance high-speed travel. This was followed in late August by the US press launch in California. A world press launch took place in France from 9 to 11 October, following the public announcement of the car on 1 October.

An interesting aside, during this last-minute build up to the public launch, was the assignment of two cars, both Convertibles, to the author and Jaguar Enthusiasts' Club General Manager Graham Searle for a two-week tour of the Jaguar dealerships in the UK, to raise money for the BEN motor industry charity. Both cars set off from Jaguar's Browns Lane Plant at the end of a Factory Open Day, one going south, the other north, picking up co-drivers en route, and they remained on the road day and night until every dealer had been visited. A total of £12,000 was raised, and the run culminated at the NEC Birmingham International Motor Show on Press Day, where the cars were handed back to Jaguar and the cheque for the money raised for BEN was given to Managing Director Nick Scheele.

Although the public announcement of the XK8 had taken place on 1 October this was only to the media, to whom initial road tests and full details were released in readiness for the official UK public launch at the British International Motor Show in Birmingham later that

Is it a car, or isn't it? It's actually a styling mock-up, without its own power or even an interior, shown to the press before the launch to get a 'feel' for public reaction. The author was privileged to be there and take this picture at the time, and in his own comments on TV that evening said 'It's a winner!' (Nigel Thorley)

month. At the show, the Jaguar stand displayed a British Racing Green Coupé and a Carnival Red Convertible, while there was an Ice Blue Coupé on the *Autocar* stand, this vehicle having been used

The author with others at the start of the XK8/Jaguar Enthusiasts Club 1996 BEN Charity fund-raising run, the venue being the BEN home in Rugby, Warwickshire. (Nigel Thorley)

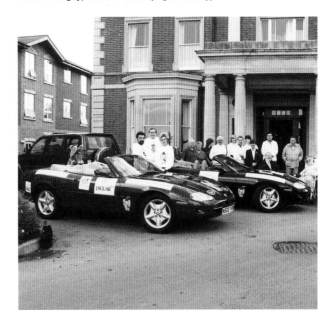

extensively for a three-way test (see below). From here on in there were launch events at all the dealerships, leading up to the British Motor Show.

It was announced that prior to the show customers had already placed orders for 5,000 XK8s, and as Jaguar only planned to produce 12,000 in the first full year of production this effectively meant a waiting list of up to five months for anyone wanting to buy one after seeing the cars at the show. As the estimated global market for grand touring sports cars was only estimated at 55,000 a year at the time, Jaguar seemed to have hit the jackpot! Cars were finally made available to UK and US dealer showrooms during October, and to the rest of the overseas markets by November.

To top it all, at the end of the year Geoff Lawson, Jaguar's Chief Designer, picked up an Italian award naming the XK8 'the world's most beautiful car'.

Shaping up to the competition

By the time it had been publicly launched, the XK8 was not the only new and exciting sporting model to hit the market. Ferrari, for example, were showing off their fabulous (and expensive) 550, while Mercedes had their spanking new small sports car, the SLK. Another expensive supercar was the Lamborghini Diablo roadster. Nor was Jaguar the only UK manufacturer to introduce a V8 sports car that year, for Lotus had their Esprit V8, which, although smaller-engined, performed admirably. Porsche had introduced their Boxster (the first totally new Porsche sports car in 18 years), TVR had their Cerbera Coupé, and Marcus introduced their 325bhp Ford-powered Mantis. Another new car, the Spectre – made in the UK and powered by a 350bhp

EARLY PERFORMANCE COMPARISONS

Car	Max bhp	Max torque	0–62 mph	Max speed	Average mpg
Jaguar XK8 Coupé	290	290	6.7sec	155mph	23
Jaguar XK8 Convertible	290	290	7.0sec	155mph	23
BMW 840 Coupé	282	310	7.1sec	155mph	20.5
Mercedes SL 320 Coupé	228	200	8.1sec	149mph	25.7
Mercedes SL 500 Convertible	326	332	5.9sec	155mph	16.2
Porsche 911 Carrera	282	251	6.4sec	168mph	23.2
Aston Martin DB7	335	360	5.8sec	157mph	19.2
Ferrari 550	484	419	4.4sec	199mph	12.3
Lexus SC400 (US only)	260	270	7.7sec	145mph	23
XJS 4.0 litre Convertible	238	282	8.0sec	145mph	21.7

Ford V8 engine – threatened the top-end sports car market. On top of all this there was existing competition from the group's own Aston Martin DB7, which although it used the old XJ-S platform at that time would soon adopt the modified XK8 pan with suspension and steering. In addition there were the Maserati Ghibli Coupé, Mercedes SL, Porsche 911, TVR Griffith, and such American contenders as the Corvette, Camaro and Viper.

What the press and the people said

'Never mind the bollocky XJS – here's Jaguar's next sexy pistol' was the opening strapline from Martin Padgett in *Car & Driver* magazine when they first got shots of the then still to be announced XK8 in 1995. A few months later, also before the public launch, *Performance Car* magazine wrote: 'Say farewell to the flabby old XJS and hello to the dynamic new V8-engined XK8, the sports car that picks up where the E-type left off.'

Autocar magazine put on quite a splash in their issue of 6 March 1996. The XK8 was featured on the front cover with the strapline 'How Jaguar Recreated a Legend', and no less than 12 pages were devoted to the new car. The carefully selected styling shots didn't reveal a great deal of detail, particularly of the interior, and no detailed specification was available at this time,

COMPARISON PERSPECTIVE

1961	Aston Martin DB4	£4,084
	Jaguar E-type Fhc	£2,196 – 54% of the Aston
1996	Aston Martin DB7	£82,500
	Jaguar XK8 Coupé	£47,950 – 58% of the Aston
1961	Aston Martin DB4	141mph top speed, 0–60 in 8.5 seconds
	Jaguar E-type	149mph top speed, 0–60 in 7.1 seconds
1996	Aston Martin DB7	157mph top speed, 0–60 in 5.8 seconds
	Jaguar XK8	155mph top speed, 0–60 in 6.6 seconds

but *Autocar* did show a number of styling drawings covering the build-up to the final design.

After the car's Geneva launch in March, the American *Road & Track* magazine got their turn to feature the XK8 Convertible in May, with an impressive six-page spread straplined 'The long wait is over … and the car is worth the wait.' It wasn't until November of that year, however, that they actually got their hands on a car (another Coupé) for a road test. In their opening remarks the phrases 'as British as Buckingham Palace', 'a Jaguar that doesn't feed off the Ford parts bin trough', and 'an unqualified stunner', set the scene. Moving on to the actual driving characteristics, they found the XK8 to be unflappable compared to the ageing XJS, with well-controlled roll, although concrete expansion joints in US roads produced annoying jolts felt through the seats. Unlike the XJS, they found the XK8 positively encouraged you to press on down twisty roads. They went into raptures over the interior's wonderful textures that appealed to the eyes and fingertips. Interestingly (and in contrast to my personal experience and those of other road-testers of more than normal height), they considered there was ample headroom and seat movement for the driver. In conclusion, they felt Jaguar was on a winner!

On 3 July *Autocar* had another major feature on Jaguar. Though not primarily covering the XK8, it did seem to have inside information about the success of the Jaguar V8 engine in Ford's eyes, so much so that the company had been given permission to carry out development work on V6 versions of the power unit of 2.0-litre and 3.0-litre capacities. They also intimated that smaller V6-engined versions of the XK8 would be made available in the future. In the same issue they speculated that a supercharged V8 was under development and would appear as the XKR8 in late 1997. They also intimated that a couple of years further on there would be another all-new XK8, smaller and sportier – but such things were speculation at the time.

The British *Autocar* magazine, who have always had a close relationship with Jaguar, were first to hit the magazine-stands with their issue of 2 October containing a ten-page road test of the Coupé accompanied by a 64-page booklet on the background to the car. They favoured its brutally elegant looks, very strong engine and gearbox combination, fluid handling, grip, price, and its quietness compared to the Aston Martin DB7 they had previously tested (which, of course, still utilised a highly modified version of the old Jaguar straight six AJ16 power plant). On the other

The monthly magazines had a field day when the XK8 was launched, in some cases issuing booklets specifically about the new car. (Nigel Thorley collection)

hand, however, they did initially find faults – fidgety low-speed ride, disappointing interior quality, and the inevitably cramped rear seats.

In a subsequent issue of *Autocar*, after the road test, some of the comments from readers make interesting reading: 'The instruments remind me of those in a 1975 Austin Princess 1800HL'; 'The front and rear three-quarter angle photographs show the obvious design influence – not E-type but Mazda MX-5!'; 'I have one minor criticism – the badge on the nose will make it awkward to attach a stick-on number plate'; 'There is something about the performance of the XK8 that is strangely familiar. Its top speed, fuel consumption and acceleration to 100mph are all so close to the E-type that to differentiate between the two cars is superfluous. Further comparison reveals that, beyond the magic ton, the E-type has the upper hand, being 3 seconds faster to 100mph. And using the E-type price of 1961, suitably adjusted, the XK8 should cost around half its £47,000. Does this latest Jaguar demonstrate the progress that is to be expected from 35 years of automotive technological advancement. I think not, but I might be persuaded to change my mind.' In April 1996 *Car* magazine commented: 'Mercedes is bracing itself for a big sales attack on the SL. The Germans, like Jaguar, believe the XK8 is bound to be a winner.'

At the end of October 1996 *Autocar* got to grips with the XK8 in a full-blown road-test Coupé. They were obviously impressed, particularly with the engine/gearbox relationship in terms of smoothness and refinement; the flawless gearchanges were compared to the very best from the likes of BMW. In

WIN AN XK FOR A WEEKEND

In November 1996 *Autocar* magazine ran a competition for a lucky reader to win an XK8 Coupé for a weekend. All you had to do was tell them the cubic capacity of the V8 engine in the XK – pretty simple really, particularly when on the next page of the spread they told you!

The *Autocar* 1996 promotion to win an XK8 for a weekend. (Reprinted from *Autocar*)

overall terms they graded the XK8 by means of points out of five: they gave it five for performance, only three for economy (though stating that it was better than the competition), four for handling and ride (having expected the top-end model with 18in wheels to be a

little firmer), but only three for comfort, equipment and safety, because the interior was fussy and created too many reflections, there was a severe lack of rear seat legroom, there wasn't enough rearward movement for the driver's seat, and there was too much Ford switchgear! As for design and engineering, the engine got full marks, but the car only got three stars because of patchy build quality. In terms of its market and cost, *Autocar* considered the XK an undoubted success, but gave it only four stars: 'Jaguar has pulled off a masterstroke with the XK8's positioning and pricing. If it can nip those last build gremlins in the bud, it'll have a winner.'

In conclusion *Autocar* commented that the XK8 had one of the best drivetrains they had driven at any price, and that it was a cracking good car to drive. The fit and finish, the styling, paintwork, etc, made it every inch the class act it promised to be. However, the lack of rear seat accommodation meant it was not really a 2+2, and the mixed quality of the interior package didn't help in allaying concerns about Jaguar's ability to produce an exceptionally high quality car. Their final ranking was four stars out of five – 'The Best GT in the Real World'.

A few weeks later *Autocar* published another report, a direct comparison of the XK8 with the more expensive Aston Martin DB7 and, although extravagantly more costly, the Ferrari 550 Maranello. Their opening statement perhaps confirmed the reason why you would pay so much more for a Ferrari than a Jaguar: 'Drive an XK8 hard enough to keep a 550 in sight and you'll soon discover weaknesses in its body control and handling, and in its brakes. Do the same in the Aston and,

XK8 as it was launched, here seen in Ice Blue with Oatmeal Classic interior and 17in Revolver wheels. (Nigel Thorley)

although the feeling will be underlaid by a keener sense of competition, you'll still leave the arena exhausted by comparison, not to mention well beaten.'

The test went badly for the XK8: 'Despite being wooed by the XK8's exquisite engine and gearbox, and by its serene cabin and near effortless motorway gait, neither of us emerged at Brescia prepared to extol its virtues with anything greater than mild enthusiasm.' The testers found the Aston quicker, quieter and more comfortable if more thirsty, and were seduced by the DB's curvaceous lines when directly compared to the XK8. The Ferrari had it all, down to image, outright performance, and handling, but at around three times the price of the Jag what else would you expect?

Similarly, they preferred the Aston to the Jag overall, and felt that the differences were significant enough to warrant the existence of the DB7, but they failed to consider whether the extra £34,000 of the latter was justified. In all an interesting but perhaps relatively inappropriate comparison of three cars aimed at very different markets.

In November, *Car* magazine's full road-test report on the XK8 stated: 'this car oozes presence and desirability. Better still it looks like a Jag and nothing else.' In their closing statement, they praised Jaguar for the new car, claiming it to be a true successor to the E-type and proof that Jaguar was anything but moribund!

There were comparisons with the competition in most of the car magazines, initially against the muscular Mercedes SL500 and, of course, the DB7. *Autocar* thought the Aston to be stylistically better and dynamically a superior car, while the XK8 had refinement, superb panel fit, and more grand touring ability. But the Jaguar showed superior agility to the Mercedes, which also looked aged in the styling department. They also identified the Mercedes to have a more integrally strong structure than the others, despite the fact it was a convertible while the others were coupés.

Another joint test between the XK8, DB7 and the BMW 840i in *Car* magazine revealed the XK8 to be by far the better car overall. They said: 'It wins because it looks, goes, handles and rides the best (it raises the game here), and costs the least by a substantial margin. Here is a proper sporting Jaguar, which we haven't seen for so long that people have forgotten what some Jaguars once were ... The BMW is yesterday's car, desirability tarnished against that of the sensual Jaguar. The Aston Martin, sad to say, is revealed as a pointless purchase at £82,500, especially when the £48,000 XK8

This XK8 Convertible is finished in the launch colour of Antigua Blue with Ivory interior and 18in Flute wheels. (Nigel Thorley)

betters it in every way.' *Motor Sport* also did a comparison test of the XK8 against the BMW 840Ci, and concluded that the Jaguar out-performed, out-handled and outclassed the Beamer!

Perhaps *Autocar* summed it up best with their end-of-year review of the cars they had tested. Against the nearest comparison sports cars the XK8 came out well: the Aston DB7 was described as 'better than a Mercedes SL in virtually all respects', the Lotus Esprit V8 as a 'stunningly quick but curiously disappointing version of the Esprit', and the TVR Cerbera as giving 'massive performance' and being 'good around corners. A real giant killer.' But the Jaguar XK8 was considered 'the most desirable GT car in the real world, by far.'

There were no complaints about the design of the hood arrangement, so often a problem for car stylists. Karmann had done an excellent job without major protrusions and, of course, the now standard and still unique feature of a full-glass heated rear screen. (Nigel Thorley)

Above: Every new car has to go through numerous crash tests and this is one XK8 that survived the ordeal very well and was subsequently used for display purposes. (Nigel Thorley)

Below: The remains of an XK8 that was subjected to a severe roll-over yet look how the centre cabin area has remained substantially intact. (Nigel Thorley)

One of Jaguar's 'spaceship' mileage test car hacks, which is now, just as you see it here, in the hands of the Jaguar Daimler Heritage Trust. (Nigel Thorley)

An interesting concept drawing for an XK8 Estate car. Lynx, a private company in the south of England, produced excellent Estate (Eventer) versions of the XJS, so why not the XK8? (Nigel Thorley collection)

Chapter **Four**

R-rated

A lot happened at Jaguar in 1996, the launch year of the XK8. Nick Scheele, the then Chairman and Chief Executive, was awarded the Midlands Businessman of the Year award, while prior to the actual launch of the new car there occurred the untimely death of David

Boole, the company's Director of Communications and Public Affairs. Joe Greenwell took David's place and saw the project through to completion. Ironically, after subsequently becoming Chief Executive of Jaguar Joe Greenwell also saw the very last XK8 come off the line in 2005.

First-hand report

As already mentioned, in the early days of the XK8 the author was lucky enough to be involved in a charity run which involved covering an extraordinary number of miles in just two weeks in one of these new cars, and the experience eventually led to me purchasing one for myself. What follows is a subjective report on my findings after driving in what was essentially a pre-production car. For example, although the standard of fit and finish was significantly improved over an XJ40 saloon or XJS, there was still some orange-peel effect to the paintwork around the boot lid area. Also, a lack of forethought meant that regular use of the boot left finger-marks all over the paintwork, and having to use the key each time to open the boot from the outside was both annoying and awkward. I was also unimpressed by the blandness of the rear end: a simple chrome finisher to the number plate area would have helped. Both this and my complaint about the boot's key operation were addressed by Jaguar later.

Aesthetically, I didn't like then, nor do I now, the exposed weld area visible on the sill below the doors – would it have been so costly to fill this in neatly before painting? At the front the positioning of the number plate seemed intrusive, another matter that both Jaguar and after-market suppliers have tried to rectify since.

Returning to matters of quality, very early on in the marathon one of the headlights got filled with condensation, a common problem still faced by many

LARGER THAN LIFE

Unipart, Jaguar's parts distributor, commissioned a special XK8 hot air balloon from Cameron Balloons of Bristol at a cost of over £100,000 for the launch of the car. This measured 69ft high and 46ft wide, with a capacity of 120,000cu ft, a top speed of 13mph, an acceleration time of 0 to 60ft in 9 seconds and a maximum rate of climb of 400ft per minute. Unfortunately, if parking were needed it would occupy the equivalent of 39 XK8 spaces!

The Unipart XK8 hot-air balloon, all 120,000cu ft of it – looking for a space to park? (Nigel Thorley collection)

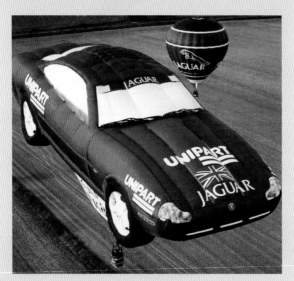

owners. The glovebox internal shelf rattled and the lid didn't fit very well. In the engine bay the plastic covers for items like the brake servo also didn't fit well, nor have they on XKs since! A particular annoyance involved the electric window lifts, the 'logic' failing four times, resulting in the window glass not raising at all, and every time you opened and closed the door, the glass dropped a further 15mm. Easy to reset, it was obviously a glitch in this particular car.

Finally, the retracting hood and its leather clad tonneau cover. The boot space proved very useful over the two weeks' journey, but then, on the road all the time, with varying weather conditions, the hood was up and down constantly, and to prevent ingress of dirt onto the headlining you had to fit the tonneau – a pain! However, it seemed to be made slightly too small for its purpose so never actually fitted properly (another common complaint), and some of the toggles that secured the tonneau in place under the boot lid actually fell off.

As regards comfort, I awarded the car seven out of ten. Despite being 6ft 2in in height I was able to find a comfortable position, but arguably there wasn't quite enough legroom, particularly for taller drivers than I. Certainly in my case, with the seat at its limit, no space was left at all for rear occupants, no matter how young and small they might have been. Also, although the seats had height adjustment, they didn't drop low enough for most tall drivers.

All the controls felt easily to hand and were comfortable and precise to use, although I had reservations about the deeply imbedded instruments in front of the driver that didn't quite look 'Jaguarish'. Visibility was also good, particularly with the top down, when the furled hood rested quite flat. One criticism was the fact you had to hold down the button to raise or lower the hood – I never understood why, when a one-touch operation would have been easier.

It took me a few miles to get used to driving the XK8. Initially it felt like any modern Jaguar, quiet, refined, and with that ambience of luxury. Under power, however, the car was much more responsive, and the steering more reactive. With its agility of handling and, of course, the amazing smoothness of the V8, I was sold! Two minor criticisms: not enough sound – under hard acceleration there was that slight V8 burble from the exhaust, but it needed something else to liven up the senses; and secondly there was a degree of lag when pressing the accelerator pedal to kick-down. Fuel consumption was good, averaging over 23mpg on the

Jaguar's obligatory 'two sets of golf clubs' boot for the XK8 worked well. The floor is shown in the lowered position with a space-saver spare wheel underneath. With a 17in Revolver wheel the floor can be raised level with the battery cover on the right-hand side, but larger wheels cannot be accommodated easily. This early car is also equipped with the CD auto-changer, on the right-hand side. (Nigel Thorley)

whole trip, which took in varying degrees of driving style by several co-drivers, plus stop-starts, demonstration runs, and so on. On one occasion I managed over 30mpg on a long cruise-controlled run up the A9 into Scotland.

Boom time

Immediately after the XK8's launch the dealers got their first cars for distribution to their new owners. Jaguar announced that in the first month 1,825 were delivered to customers, 847 of these in the US, an all-time sales record for Jaguar sports cars in that country. Of the US cars 50 were marketed as special editions through the prestigious Norman Marcus catalogue, and all sold within 72 hours of the catalogue being produced. All this boosted Jaguar's overall sales significantly, in fact a 39 per cent increase on the same period in 1995.

AUCTION DEBUT

The XK8 made its 'used car' auction debut at British Car Auctions' Blackbush, London, auction room at the end of 1997 via a Jaguar 'closed auction' of company vehicles. A 1996 'P' registered Convertible with 12,400 miles on the clock sold for £50,000.

The first quarter's sales figures for 1997 were the best sports car sales recorded in Jaguar's history – 3,977, which was 257 per cent up on 1996, when the XJS was nearing the end of its days. In March alone, Jaguar sold 248 XKs in the UK, another record for them. By the end of 1997 the total sales for the full year amounted to 14,619, an 88 per cent increase on the previous year. A total of 49.8 per cent of these were sold in the States, and worldwide 64 per cent of all cars sold were Convertibles, a greater figure than Jaguar anticipated. Some statistics collected by Jaguar reveal a lot:

		USA	UK
Average age of XK8 buyer		55 (75% male)	49 (89% male)
Occupations	Self-employed	16%	49%
	Management	23%	19%
	Professional	26%	13%
	Retired	20%	13%
	Housewife	5%	5%

TAG Models' XK8, the first die-cast produced of the new car, coinciding with the launch of the real thing. (Nigel Thorley collection)

Late in 1997 this boot-lid mounted high-intensity brake light, obligatory in the States, became standard equipment on all new XK8s. (Nigel Thorley)

Top selling exterior colour schemes at that time were: (1) Carnival Red; (2) Anthracite (black); (3) Sapphire Blue; (4) British Racing Green; and (5) Topaz (light gold).

To keep pace with demand the shifts at the Browns Lane factory were increased, and the company turned out more cars per week than at any other time in its history (XJ saloons included).

Two major service recalls were made in 1997 and 1998, the first affecting 4,500 early build cars constructed between July and November 1996 after Jaguar themselves had experienced three incidents of rear suspension failure. The fault, which involved a retaining ring between the differential and output shaft becoming dislocated under hard cornering, was apparently caused by supplier problems, and was rectified on all the appropriate cars by dealers. The second recall affected production between July and October 1997, and involved inspecting and replacing a potentially faulty throttle cable bracket.

With the hype surrounding the 'new' XK8, it wasn't long before modelmakers got to grips with the car, and a host of toys and detailed scale models began to appear. First on the scene, within weeks of the public launch, were TAG Precision Models from Leicestershire with their highly detailed, 10in long die-cast model of the Convertible, in the launch colour of Antigua Blue with Ivory interior. In those days this model cost a whopping £62, but that was the price of up-to-the-minute exclusivity! By the end of the year the same model (made by Maisto) was on offer for a mere £15.95.

At the British International Motor Show of 1997 Jaguar introduced their XJ8 range of saloons utilising much of the technology developed for the XK, and as time went on various aspects of the two model ranges merged to clean up the parts bin. The biggest news at the time was the announcement of the new Supercharged V8 XJR saloon, and although denied at the time, it was inevitable that this engine would eventually go into the XK8, just as magazines had been predicting.

A Police XK8?

Not quite, but almost. The picture says it all, and anyone contemplating breaking the speed limit might well reconsider their actions after seeing one of these Police cars! But the truth of the matter is that not only was the XK8 too expensive for a Police vehicle but it was hardly practical either, with lack of interior accommodation or places to install all their hardware (although that large boot could arguably take a few cones). This car, a standard Carnival Red Coupé, was dressed up as a Police car and loaned to the Metropolitan Police by arrangement between Ian Jackson from that force and Jaguar's Special Vehicle Operations Department. It was used for a trip to Europe for the annual European Police Motor Clubs Conference.

Into 1998

This was the year in which the first public announcement was made of problems with the Nikasil coating used on engine bores – though not with Jaguar, but with BMW. The latter admitted to over 600 engines being changed in six months due, it was felt, to sulphur damage, thought to occur when acid generated during cold starts attacked the nickel base of the coating. Jaguar at the time denied it was a problem in their own cars, as their engines were designed for fast warm-up. However, as many now know, Jaguar suffered as well, and this is covered elsewhere in this book.

Up to this time demand and residual values of XK8s had been remarkably high, in fact the best figures Jaguar had achieved in many a year. But with the car approaching two years of age, and after the successful introduction of the big V8-engined saloons (particularly

Caught on camera: not something the average motorist would want to see on the roads in 1997, this is fortunately a mere 'mock-up' for the European Police Motor Clubs Conference. (Nigel Thorley collection)

the XJR), it was inevitable that more XKs would come onto the market second-hand. By early 1998 this had resulted in a significant downturn in used car prices by up to £3,000, particularly on Coupés, and there became a strong differentiation in demand for specific specifications. In each of two consecutive months the British used car guides dropped XK prices by 3 per cent.

Enter the R

It had long been known that eventually a more powerful version of the XK8 would be made available, in order for Jaguar to keep abreast of the competition. Once the XJ8 saloons had been announced in 1997, including the XJR 4.0-litre Supercharged V8 model, it was inevitable that the same engine would make its way into the sports car – and that car went on sale in May 1998 as the XKR, available in both Coupé and Convertible forms. Jaguar's fastest-selling sports car was set to also become the fastest performing sports car in their history. The first

The XKR at launch, both Convertible and Coupé being in the special XKR-only colour (at the time) of Phoenix Red. (Nigel Thorley collection)

announcement of the XKR was made a few weeks before the Geneva Motor Show, the long-established launch pad for sporting Jaguars, where it arrived just in time to commemorate the 50th anniversary of the XK120, Jaguar's first post-war sports car.

As with the XK8 at the Geneva event of 1996, a special launch colour was chosen, then only available for the R models. This was Phoenix Red, echoing, although not exactly the same hue as, the Carmen Red used on E-types in the 1960s. The complete range of XKR exterior colour schemes was very limited at first, and didn't even include Spindrift White, a popular colour in overseas markets, because there were fears

The special bonnet louvres – a throwback to E-type days – had a purpose, helping to keep the engine cool. Initially you couldn't buy them or an XKR bonnet pressing unless you already owned this model. (Nigel Thorley)

For the supercharged model, out went the chromed splitter bar and in came a mesh grille. A subtle badge change on the nose also identified this model. (Nigel Thorley)

that the heat generated under-bonnet would discolour the exterior paintwork over time.

At a casual glance the XKR looked little different to a conventional XK8, but there were subtle changes. Starting at the front, a stainless steel mesh grille occupied the nose area, reminiscent of that used on XJR saloons from 1994, a feature that has become the norm on all Jaguar high performance vehicles since. A new badge adorned the nose, now reading 'Jaguar Supercharged', the same treatment also appearing on the boot lid.

The bonnet pressing, although the same as the XK8, carried two inset louvred panels to aid airflow and keep the under-bonnet area cool. Strategically positioned for the best low pressure airflow, they also reflected the style of the E-type bonnet. The bonnet pressing had to be adapted to allow for the movement of stiffeners and a new sound-deadening liner was fitted to accommodate the louvres.

On the boot lid a small and discrete spoiler was fitted which was apparently not only for adornment but also aided airflow, compensating the aerodynamics for the addition of the bonnet louvres, all the aerodynamic aspects being tested in a wind tunnel. Finally, new 'XKR' badging appeared at the rear. An interesting aspect was that Jaguar would not supply the rear spoiler or louvred bonnet as after-market parts except for bona fide XKR cars.

New wheels and tyres were adopted to handle the increased performance. The alloy wheels, called

Double Fives (ie ten spokes), had 8in rims at the front and 9in at the rear. All the wheels were fitted with red background growler centre-cap badges, at that time unique to the XKR. Pirelli P-Zero System tyres were again used, this time 245/45 ZR 18 at the front and 255/45 ZR 18 at the rear. Of a revised construction, they suited the car well, improving both handling and grip and providing a new linear response to steering inputs.

Easy to miss at first glance, but the XKR benefited from a separate rear spoiler on the boot lid. Note too the extra badge, which was deleted a little later. (Nigel Thorley)

The new **Double Five** alloy wheel with red centre for the XKR model. (Nigel Thorley)

Mechanically the XKR was significantly based on the new XJR V8 saloon announced earlier. With much of the development work done and the saloon in production (and selling well) it was a straight

The supercharged engine installation in the XKR. (Nigel Thorley)

carryover of technology into the XKR. It featured, for example, a variant of the existing 4.0-litre AJ-V8 supercharged engine first seen in the XJ8 the year before. Essentially the same unit with minor changes to accommodate the different location, the ECUs were recalibrated to the sports car specification. With the Eaton M112 supercharger fitted and a compact air-to-liquid intercooling system with twin intercoolers, it generated the same 370bhp, providing an excellent 28 per cent increase in power over the normally aspirated XK8 engine with a 33 per cent increase in available torque.

An even more efficient radiator and condenser were fitted and a modified exhaust system, to meet legislation and cut down noise levels. A new run of pipework to suit the gearbox (see below) fitted to supercharged cars and the downpipes and heatshields were also unique to R models. Unlike the normally aspirated cars, with one fuel pump, XKR models used two fuel pumps with revised pipework, an installation again taken from the equivalent saloon model developed earlier.

With the extra power output from the supercharged V8 engine, Jaguar chose a new heavy-duty transmission, the Mercedes W5A 580 five-speed, electronically controlled, intelligent automatic. Beefier than the ZF XK8 unit, it required revised mountings.

The XKR was the first car in the world to feature the new ZF Servotronic Mark 2 speed-sensitive power assisted steering system. Its variable ratio rack was recalibrated to provide a greater degree of weighting at medium to high speeds, improving steering response and precision and providing more feel during cornering. Steering response under all conditions was also improved by the use of stiffer mounting bushes. A new rack was mounted on a revised crossmember.

As the XJ8 owed a lot of its suspension and brake development to the XK8, the enhanced systems used on the XJR were followed through to the XKR. This included the fitment of a two-piece propshaft and upgrades in the suspension to cope with the increased performance. All XKR models were fitted as standard with the Jaguar CATS electronically controlled suspension system. Upgraded front disc brake pads, of lead-free construction, were fitted to cope with anticipated higher working temperatures.

Unseen changes included many modifications to the wiring harnesses and allied systems to accommodate the new engine and transmission. A new cross-brace

Important new elements of the XKR – the Eaton supercharger and the Mercedes gearbox. (Nigel Thorley collection)

At first glance there was little difference between XK8 and XKR interiors. But all XKRs had Sport trim as standard and carried the 'XKR' insignia embossed onto the steering wheel boss. (Nigel Thorley collection)

Look a little closer and the rev counter has a revised red line calibration and carries the 'Supercharged' logo. (Nigel Thorley)

had to be used at the front on Convertible models, to ease the fitment and removal of the radiator and condenser. To improve torsional rigidity, B/C post braces were also added.

Internally, little changed for the XKR model except that, even at this higher price level, the Sports pack trim finish was standardised. However, all XKR owners got a CD auto-change, cruise control, all leather faced seats, memory mirrors and headlamp power-wash in the standard specification, and to differentiate the R

Leather seat pleating took on a different style for the XKR models. (Nigel Thorley)

from the 8 the 'XKR' logo was embossed into the half wood/leather steering wheel centre and there was a discrete 'Supercharged' legend in the main instrumentation. The rev counter was also recalibrated to match the increased performance of the engine.

In the UK the XKR Coupé cost £60,005 and the Convertible £67,005. The extra £9,350 over the equivalent normally aspirated engined XK8s did include a £4,000 value of additional equipment, an extra cost on the other models.

With the increasing popularity of the Jaguar marque in Germany – in fact Jaguar had experienced an incredible 2,000 per cent increase in sales there since the introduction of the XK8 – a celebration saw the first 50 lucky owners of XKRs flown over to the UK to personally collect their cars. Arriving at the Jaguar factory, they were given a tour of the production facility, wined and dined, before collecting their cars (over £3 million worth) to drive back to Germany the next day.

Comparative performances

	bhp	Torque	0–60 mph	Top speed	Price
Jaguar XKR Coupé	370	387	5.1sec	155mph	£60,000
Porsche 911 Carrera	296	251	5.6sec	171mph	£65,000
Honda NSX	276	220	5.7sec	170mph	£69,500
Lotus Esprit V8	349	295	4.2sec	172mph	£59,950
Nissan Skyline GTR	280	271	5.0sec	155mph	£50,000
Chevrolet Corvette	339	356	5.7sec	171mph	£39,000
Chrysler Viper GTS	378	454	5.3sec	151mph	£68,800
TVR Cerbera V8	420	380	4.3sec	185mph	£45,000
Aston Martin DB7	317	337	6.9sec	155mph	£82,500

More press comments

In 1997 *Autocar* magazine took two examples of the XK8 to RAF Coltishall for a photo-shoot with the Jaguar GR1 jet fighter planes based there. As if anyone needed confirmation of the success of the XK8, all the RAF personnel were totally seduced by the cars (a matching Coupé and Convertible) – as their Wing Commander put it: 'It's simply stunning, prettier than a DB7, and yet classic Jaguar. I want one.'

A little later Steve Cropley enjoyed a Convertible in Wales, commenting that it was one of the finest top-down cruisers to glide off a production line anywhere in the world. After reporting earlier on the Coupé version he was apprehensive about the structural rigidity of the Convertible and its practicalities. Given that the weather was terrible and the car was not equipped with CATS suspension or the larger 18in wheels, he was exceptionally pleased with it. He further stated there was no downside to a Convertible, even if it cost another £7,000 (which you got back in resale value down the line).

Autocar also had a long-term loan XK8 Coupé from Jaguar, and in August 1997, after 7,500 miles, reported that it was 'truly special' and that 'dynamically our long-term Jaguar XK8 has never failed to impress'.

Criticisms amounted to the lack of interior space: they felt it really wasn't a 2+2 at all because they couldn't get two people of the correct size and shape to fit the rear seat. They would also have liked Jaguar to drop the variable ratio steering, and didn't like the accelerator pedal, which required lots of prodding to get the best out of the performance: even in kick-down the response was slow. Just two months later the car had covered 15,000 miles and their respect for it continued to grow. Fellow journalist from *Motor Sport* Andrew Frankel got hold of the car for a European trip and managed to notch up an indicated 161mph on the speedometer, probably very close to the 155mph maximum speed that Jaguar publicised, and he found it perfectly stable and could still carry out a normal conversation in the cockpit.

Throughout the total mileage the only problem thus far had been the loss of one of the headlamp pressure wash covers. Their summing up said: 'Great shape, fine engine, suspension, performance, handling, effortless mile-eating ability with surprising fuel consumption. A fine car which gains stature with the miles and underlines Jaguar's new reputation for building cars

On the docks: a lucky German XKR owner taking his new car home. (Nigel Thorley collection)

	UK	USA	Europe	RoW	Total
1996	945	2,183	789	356	4,273
1997	2,817	7,223	3,412	1,049	14,501
1998	2,913	6,189	3,210	607	12,919
1999	1,912	6,449	3,032	447	11,840

well. Rakish looks go with top-drawer road ability but belie XK8's easy to own nature. Great value against the competition.'

At 20,000 miles new brake pads and new front brake discs were called for because of a slight judder at slow speed; this was done under warranty. They also replaced the rear tyres. Another 5,000 miles down the line the front tyres had also worn down and a brake light bulb needed replacement.

At 35,000 miles the car came in for replacement, and the other problems experienced were summarised. These, in the main, were very minor, from an intermittent front suspension clunk, to the headlining drooping, the wipers stopping working, a facia rattle, and a boot lid that at one time didn't or wouldn't close. Other than these they had nothing but praise for the car, and the total costs incurred over 35,000 miles only amounted to £1,701.47 for service and parts.

Autosport also had the opportunity, for a week, to compare the XK8 Coupé with the equivalent Mercedes SL500, and their comments are worth reproducing in full: 'The Jag has a more rigid, better-riding body. Its facia is simpler, better laid out and – surprise – its switches and controls have more of a quality feel. And I liked its driving position better. The Benz, on the other hand, had a truly brilliant powertrain. No smoother or quieter than the XK8's, but torquier, more responsive at low revs, and driving through a slicker, quicker-acting transmission.'

Views of the car were, as always, somewhat subjective. For example, *Car Trends* magazine said after testing a Convertible that they thought the steering was heavy and vague, but praised the brakes. When *What Car?* magazine first tried the XK8 they concluded that it wasn't an aggressive muscle car welcoming boastful driving, nor was it the last word in handling and performance, but it was seductive, nimble and quick, and nothing remotely came close in price. *Top Gear* magazine got their chance to try the XK8 in 1997 in a direct comparison with the BMW M3, Porsche 911 and Mercedes SL320, driving all three on the Continent to establish their 'grand touring' abilities. They obviously favoured the Porsche but stated that the Jag had the grand touring balance right, while both the Porsche and BMW supplied the better driving fun.

Autocar got first crack of the whip with the XKR Coupé via Mark Hughes, who commented early on in his report that 'the sheer thrust from 2,000 to 6,000rpm is not only awesome and untemperamental, but also relentless', and finished with the comment: 'combines XK8's refinement and comfort with truly fearsome performance.' Later that year the same magazine carried out a head-to-head between an XKR Convertible and the equivalent Porsche 911 Carrera Convertible. Similarly priced, the Jaguar had the edge in performance, comfort, ride and boot space, but the Porsche was decidedly the better drivers' car.

In an *Autocar* ranking of 1998 cars the XKR came a lowly 47th out of 100, supposedly based on its fuel consumption, brakes and handling. They also carried out a Britain's Best Drivers' Car test at around the same time, in which the XKR came woefully far down the list because they felt it was more of a grand touring car than sports. It was, however, in good company at the bottom, with the Prodrive Imprezza. The Jaguar managed a lap time around Silverstone of 1min 15.15sec compared to the Porsche 911 at 1min 12.12sec and the Lotus Esprit at 1min 11.60sec. Problems with the XK related to the brakes (again), lack of control from the automatic transmission, and even the traction control.

Car magazine also did a major head-to-head, with the XKR pitched against the DB7, BMW 840Ci, Mercedes SL60, Porsche 911, and the Nissan NSX and Skyline, a formidable bunch. Looking for the best all-rounder, they straight away ruled out the SL on the basis of cost/value for money and lack of driver feel. The Skyline was dropped for its brashness and cheapness! The BMW felt like an old car, was too big and wasn't the best at anything. The Aston was a good all-rounder but too expensive and apparently flawed in many areas. The second Nissan was then discarded on the basis of style and steering, which left the Porsche and Jaguar. They loved the Porsche and thought it a very exciting car, but the XKR won the day for so many reasons, not least because 'the Jaguar handles the drama for you so your drive will be more relaxing … The Jaguar's monstrous, relentless torque is wholly addictive and completely thrilling, but you can arrive at your destination unshaken even though you have been stirred.'

Chapter Five

Ongoing development and excitement

With sales buoyant after an upsurge resulting from the addition of the two new XKR models, Jaguar and the XK were flying high. The production figures up to the end of 1998 were the same as sales, as Jaguar was selling every XK it produced:

	1997	1998
XK8 Coupé	5,141	3,319
XK8 Convertible	9,765	7,662
XKR Coupé	11	1,402
XKR Convertible	12	838
Totals	14,929	13,221

Rumours abounded during 1998 that Jaguar was up to something in the form of an even quicker version of the XKR, a new car that would appear at one of the international motor shows. The press and public were not to be disappointed when, at the Paris Motor Show in September 1998, Jaguar unveiled the XK180 to rapturous applause. Although at the time a non-runner (later it would actually run, and still does), Jaguar boss Nick Scheele stated that within months a street-legal version would be built.

The XK180 is definitely a part of the XK8 story, as it is significantly based on the then still new XKR, and many of its features were later incorporated into XK

To create a concept car like the XK180 required many hours of hand crafting and finishing, to achieve what turned out to be a superb result. (Nigel Thorley)

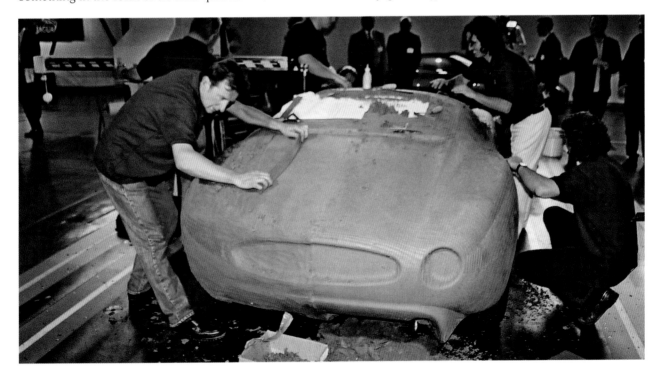

production. Although very much a concept car it paved the way for later XK development and led to its eventual replacement by the aluminium-bodied car.

Special Vehicle Operations

The XK180 story started with the formation of a new department within Jaguar, Special Vehicle Operations, a spin-off from the Limousine Department that used to manufacture the Daimler DS420 at Browns Lane. Rather than lose such expertise following the demise of that model, the SVO Department was set up, primarily to provide bespoke modifications to existing models and carry out development work and support in the provision of specialist vehicles like Police cars, one-off prototypes, and such things as armour-plated cars.

To give the department greater exposure, the idea developed – with approval from Jaguar's directors – that it should also work on other projects, such as special trim adaptations to customer specifications, and out of this came the Insignia project, which offered interior and exterior trim mods on the XJ40 saloons and XJS sports models that were relatively successful in their own way. Later the department worked on the Daimler Corsica concept two-door drophead coupé, based on the X-300 saloon, built to commemorate 100 years of Daimler motor cars. The scene was therefore set for SVO to get involved in other projects based on current vehicles.

The most powerful AJ-V8 engine up to that time, installed in the XK180. (Nigel Thorley)

The XK180 was originally conceived in 1997, when it was envisaged as a mildly modified XKR but with a vastly uprated engine and some styling add-ons from Jaguar's D-type racing era. However, with the help of Keith Helfet, from the Jaguar styling team (who had previously been involved in such diverse projects as the XJS facelift, the XJ220 supercar and, of course, the XK8), this idea soon developed into producing the ultimate XKR sports car. Once that was agreed the decks were cleared and the opportunity was taken to lighten the car – effectively to totally redesign it, designing and building an entirely new body structure from aluminium.

Using the 1950s D-type as inspiration and the production XK8 as a base to produce a viable modern car, not just a rehash of something that had gone before, work began in earnest. It was felt important that the origins of the XK8 should show through, but the project gave the team the opportunity to shorten the relatively long wheelbase and rear overhang and incorporate modern styling ideas which would also be functional.

A hack of an XK8 Convertible was chosen for development. SVO cut the shell to remove 5in of wheelbase, fitted a strong roll-over cage, and set to work on the other aspects of design with the help of Jaguar's Whitley Engineering facility. From Helfet's original drawings, Abbey Panels Limited in Coventry (who used to produce the Jaguar E-type bonnet, XJ220 shells, and much more) built a clay styling buck onto which the aluminium body was hand rolled and beaten. Meanwhile back at the SVO department at Browns Lane, an XKR platform was prepared, shortened by 125mm, onto which the hand-built body was fitted and the rest of the car was built up. The end product turned out to be actually 345mm shorter than the production XK because of other styling changes at the front and rear. There had not been sufficient time or money to go in for any stringent testing – even the body wasn't wind-tunnel tested.

As for the mechanics, the XKR parts bin was raided, but racing-style adjustable Bilstein aluminium shock absorbers were mounted inside the uprated adjustable coil springs. The enhanced braking system came from Brembo, with larger cross-drilled ventilated discs and aluminium four-pot callipers. The anti-roll bars, all bushes and the rear A-frame to support the suspension were also strengthened. Steering was pure XKR but with higher gearing.

The standard five-speed Mercedes automatic transmission from the XKR was fitted, but not with the

From any angle the proportions of the XK180 look right, and the XK8 connections are obvious. (Nigel Thorley)

usual J-gate operation. Instead, Jaguar opted to fit a 'slick-shift' type of button gear-change system via the steering wheel. An indication on the dash alerted the driver to which gear was selected.

The biggest news came with the engine installation. The then current 4.0-litre V8 Supercharged engine found in the XKR and XJR models was again used as its base, but with modifications to the Supercharger gearing speed (increasing it by 10 per cent), a bigger intercooler, improved induction, and big-bore exhaust system. Jaguar were able to extract a whopping 450bhp out of the engine with approximately 445lb of torque. The rest of the drive-train was pure XKR. To transit that performance to the road, massive 20in split-rim alloy wheels were fitted, 9in wide at the front, 10in at the rear, with Pirelli P-Zero tyres.

The end result of the XK180 styling was and still is quite amazing, particularly considering that the whole project was built and brought to launch in just 12 months without formal technical drawings and with such a small team involved. Externally the car still owes much to the XKR – the imposing front with obligatory mesh grille – but the revised bonnet design (opening à la E-type, with enlarged louvres to dissipate the heat) and the slightly 'stubbed' nose makes it look more purposeful. The smooth side lines, without door handles, and the upswept nature of the doors leading into the rear wings, are clean and pleasing to the eye

yet retain much of the XK in their design. The shortened wheelbase also suits the car well. The sculptured treatment to the rear deck, echoing the seat headrests, looks wonderful, and the rear spoiler does its job so much better than the D-types fins of the 1950s. Helfet even chose an evocative, yet technologically advanced metallic paint finish for the car, apparently taking cues from the 1957 Le Mans winning Ecurie Ecosse D-types and the traditional British Racing Green.

Although the team started with a slightly modified XKR set-up, the internal styling also developed into something exciting but always functional, with strong use of aluminium and leather and the reversion to toggle-type switches and, not least, the lovely red starter button. Front seats are Recaro with proper full racing harnesses, but there is no room for rear seating because of the reduced wheelbase, and the car is all the better for it.

Yes, the XK180 was a pure concept car meant to stir the imagination and generate excitement about the Jaguar brand, something it did remarkably well. But it is also fair to say that every part of the concept was viable for a production car had Jaguar the time and money to have addressed the legislative and

A very functional approach to the interior, with instrument layout taken from the 1960s Jaguar style. Note the red starter button near the gear lever. (Nigel Thorley)

The XK180 was the first Jaguar to have paddle-shift gearchange controls on the steering wheel, this very tactile gearlever change and quadrant being a theme only just coming to production in the all-alloy XK. (Nigel Thorley)

technical issues when they originally designed it. Indeed, many features from the XK180 found their way into later models. For example, the shortened wheelbase and reduced rear overhang is found in the very latest (aluminium) XK models. The improved engine performance also benefited later cars. The use of digital rear lighting found its way into the S-type saloon in 1999 and later into other Jaguar models too. The beefed-up braking system and alloys turned up on XKs not long after in the form of R-Performance options, and even the alloy dash is now an option on cars as diverse as the X-type and XJR.

Public reaction to the car was incredible, with many defying Jaguar not to build it as a production vehicle, but it was not to be. Whether because of budgetary factors, fears of another XJ220 situation, or simply a lack of sufficient resources, the project was prevented from going further.

The ultimate driving experience

Though this is a phrase used by BMW, it is one your author cares to use in relation to the XK180, having had the opportunity to drive this fabulous motorcar. The seats seem to fit every driver perfectly and there is no loss of room compared to a standard XK. The small leather clad steering wheel falls easily to hand and you have just enough controls to worry about without the cockpit being fussy – in fact it takes you back to earlier days when cars were much simpler.

Pushing that evocative red starter button bursts the engine into life, and the sound from the enlarged exhaust system needs to be bottled for permanent appreciation (TVR eat your heart out). The car feels easier and lighter to drive than the XK8 or XKR (it is 200kg lighter anyway) and you quickly feel a part of it. The seats hold you firm, the smaller diameter steering wheel gives you excellent control, and the whole car feels solid and exceptionally smooth, but the sound of that exhaust note urges you on to use the power under your right foot.

The steering is nice and sharp, much more so than the production XKs (probably because of the shorter wheelbase), and the car feels more manoeuvrable despite the massive 20in wheels connecting you to the road. The performance is excellent – better, in fact, than you actually realise – and there are no vices in the form of knocks, groans, or harshness. The XK180 is a fantastic drivers' car, and surprisingly refined as well.

You have the choice of full automatic transmission or moving the selector to 'manual', which gives you total control over gear changes via the steering wheel mounted buttons. The ease and smoothness of gear changes is a credit to the car, and judicious use of the gears enables the car to rocket to speeds unthought-of. But you have to be careful: remember that there's a lot

of horsepower under the bonnet, the wheelbase is short, and you're not a Formula One driver!

All in all a fantastic experience I shall always remember, and it's easy to see why most enthusiasts were demanding that such a beautiful car should have been built.

XK 180 performance

Top speed	180mph
0–60mph	5.0 seconds
0–100mph	10.0 seconds

1999 model year changes

The launch of the S-type and the XK180 Concept took the spotlight somewhat off other production vehicles, including the XK, despite the still comparatively recent addition of the XKR range. However, two new colour schemes were introduced for all models, Alpine Green and Emerald Green displacing Sherwood and Aquamarine from the XK range. Also, by popular demand the XKR launch colour, Phoenix Red, now became a standard production colour available on any

XK model. To complement the somewhat restricted range of colours for the XKR cars, Meteorite Silver and Topaz (gold) were offered as additional schemes. The original Stone colour option for the Convertible hood on both XK8 and XKR models was supplanted by Light Beige. (A full list of all XK colour schemes by year will be found in the appendices.)

The XK Convertible models came in for some revision. To structurally improve the integrity of the Convertible shell a stiffening brace was fitted between the seat belt pillar and the B post. To do this involved the movement and modification of quite a few ancillary items, right down to heatshields and audio speakers. This was an adaptation of the stiffening brace already fitted to XKR models. In addition an X brace was fitted at the front to aid the removal and fitting of the radiator and air conditioning condenser. Again this followed XKR practice and rationalised the production changes for all cars.

More happened 'under the skin'. Firstly, due to changing legislation over European impact requirements, the bodyshell had to be further strengthened to sustain front offset body deformation in an accident. Reinforced panels extended the driver and front passenger toeboards back towards the transmission tunnel, along with internal stiffening to the adjacent side members. On Coupé bodies additional plates were welded to the side members to further reinforce the toeboard area, and an extra stiffening panel was welded to the inside of each outer sill. In October 1998 the Mark 2 Servotronic steering system, originally adopted for the XJR and XKR, became standard fitment on all XK models.

The AJ-V8 engines of all models also came in for revision. Now coded AJ27 (the original engine was AJ26), they featured air-assisted fuel injectors that gave improved performance and reduced the time for catalysts to reach operating temperatures. On the normally aspirated engines the previous two-stage variable cam phasing gave way to a continuously variable system, which provided for a linear valve timing pattern to improve torque at low speeds and optimise emissions, while modified pistons with increased skirt length improved refinement. Finally, a more responsive electronic throttle controlled the engine management system. All the 4.0-litre engines benefited from the fitment of dual-tipped platinum spark plugs, which provided nearly 70,000 miles of service life before they needed to be changed. All these modifications were necessary to satisfy ever more

stringent regulations regarding emissions, particularly in the US. In addition the oil cooler was deleted from the specification of the normally aspirated engines.

On the supercharged engines, a new kickdown control switch gave improved response. The braking system was also enhanced for supercharged models by the fitment of larger discs and lead-free Textar brake pads. The ZF gearbox also came in for revision, with a recalibration to improve gearshift quality on non-supercharged engines.

Customers ordering new XK8 models with CATS suspension henceforward benefited from the fitment of stiffer steering bushes and Bilstein shock absorbers, like the XKR models. Similarly, if the optional 18in alloy wheels were specified the XKR-type Pirelli P-Zero tyres were fitted.

Hardly anything had changed with the external trim except that the relatively new badge on the boot lids of XKR and some overseas XK8 models was finally deleted at the end of 1998. Internally, Sport trim cars got an Ambla door trim instead of cloth finish, while the legends on the instrumentation for all models changed to make them more legible. A boot stowage net became a standard fitment in all XK models to secure small items.

As the British International Motor Show readied us for the 1999 model season, things began to hot up for

SHAPING UP TO THE COMPETITION

A comparison of the XKR with its rivals, in terms of performance and price, now read as follows:

	bhp	Torque	0–60 mph	Top speed	Price
Jaguar XKR Coupé	370	387	5.1sec	155mph	£60,010
Porsche Carrera 4	300	258	5.2sec	174mph	£67,850
Maserati 3200GT	370	362	5.1sec	164mph	£60,765
Lotus Esprit GT	349	295	4.1sec	171mph	£49,950
Chevrolet Corvette	339	356	5.3sec	165mph	£40,425
Chevrolet Cam Z28	280	332	5.4sec	158mph	£22,725
Chrysler Viper	378	454	5.3sec	172mph	£68,800
TVR Cerbera Speed 6	350	330	4.5sec	180mph	£41,100

NB: The top speed of all XKs has always been electronically limited to 155mph. However, it is known that on test at MIRA standard production XKRs have achieved up to 175mph.

the Jaguar XK. Although not direct competition, the limelight was switched to cars like the new Audi TT, Jaguar's own S-type saloon, and even the Ford Focus and Rover 75. Actual competition for the XK included the newly imported Porsche Carrera 4 Cabriolet and four-wheel drive models, Jensen's new (but stillborn) Interceptor, the AC Ace and Aceca Coupé, the entirely new Maserati 3200 GT, and Aston's Vantage, so it was a good place to show off the XK180 and attract attention to the XKR.

Depreciation was starting to finally take its toll on the XK8, a worry for both Jaguar and their dealers, for whom it was going to prove a rough winter. Values of early XK8s had dropped by over £1,000 per month. Sales had been so buoyant that it was obvious the market had to cool down as more and more second-hand cars became available. The XKs, though, held out much better than some of the competition, with long-term price-drooping models like the Range Rover suffering twice as badly as Jaguar.

Despite this, Jaguar made strong progress for the second year in succession in the annual JD Power US survey on vehicle reliability. Jaguar improved their position to become second to Subaru, although the main beneficiary of this was the XJ saloon. The XK8 still

At the British International Motor Show the XKR helped to boost sales for the XK range to level out the losses – particularly from the XK8 Coupé – of 1999. (Nigel Thorley)

came well down the list, but JD Power awarded Jaguar the Most Improved Brand award.

XK6?

After the excitement of the XK180, news leaked from Jaguar in 1999 relating to the possible development of a new, smaller sports car as an addition to the XK8 range. Sources claimed it would be launched around 2001 and would be based significantly on the then still new S-type saloon platform (also shared with the Lincoln LS in America). Using the S-type's 3.0-litre V6 engine and possibly the 4.0-litre V8 as well, it was estimated that the new XK6 would be much smaller than the XK8, have design cues from the S-type, and be designed alongside a new Ford Thunderbird to cut costs and development time.

This was, at the time, a very logical development following the success of the XK8. Jaguar needed something with which to attack the competition in this field, where cars like the Porsche Boxster, Mercedes SLK and BMW Z3 M prevailed. There were even fears

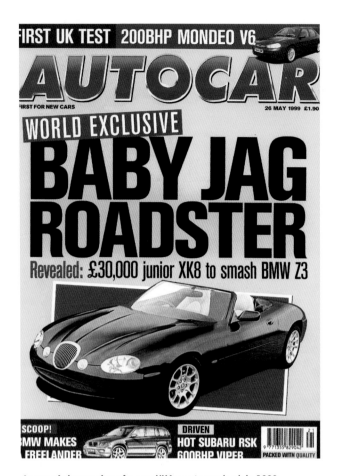

FIRST UK TEST 200BHP MONDEO V6

AUTOCAR
FIRST FOR NEW CARS   26 MAY 1999 £1.90

WORLD EXCLUSIVE

BABY JAG ROADSTER

Revealed: £30,000 junior XK8 to smash BMW Z3

SCOOP!
BMW MAKES FREELANDER

DRIVEN
HOT SUBARU RSK
600BHP VIPER

Autocar's impression of a new XK6 sports car, back in 1999.
(Reprinted from *Autocar*)

Burberry, the clothing manufacturer, had previously created special
XJ-S cars using their well-known materials. An XK8 Convertible
followed in 1999. (Nigel Thorley)

that BMW (now owners of Rover) might resurrect the Austin Healey name with a car for this market. Although, as we now know, the XK6 came to nothing, development was under way for something even better – the F-type, a project we'll return to in the next chapter.

Key personnel changes

Early in 1999 Jaguar announced that Nick Scheele, its Chairman and Chief Executive, was leaving to take up a new position with Ford as their Senior Vice-President Europe. Nick had joined the company back in April 1992 and had worked hard to see the X-100 project through. He had always been a strong supporter of the model, and of Jaguar Cars, and would again take some responsibility for Jaguar as a whole after becoming Ford's Senior Vice-President World. He was instrumental in bringing Joe Greenwell back to Jaguar as Chief Executive.

Chief Stylist Geoff Lawson died suddenly in June the same year, and was succeeded by Ian Callum, the man behind the Aston Martin DB7 who was later to design the aluminium XK that would replace the models covered in this book.

R-Performance

In readiness for the Frankfurt Motor Show in September 1999, and coinciding with Ford's decision to brand their Formula One team as Jaguar, the company finally introduced some of the add-ons first seen in the XK180 and developed under the Special Vehicle Operations banner. Primarily intended for the XK8 and XKR models, but also made available for some of the XJ range and S-types, these performance-related options by SVO were identified by the name 'R-Performance'. They were available on new cars by special order, but customers with older cars would have to wait until 2000 to get them as after-market add-ons from a Jaguar dealer.

BBS designed and supplied the R-Performance alloy wheels, which for the XK were either 18in Milan or 20in Paris or Detroit (named after the launch venues for the XK180 concept car), all of the two-piece, split-rim make-up. The 20in wheels were the largest ever to be fitted to a Jaguar car. All wheels were fitted with very low-profile Pirelli P-Zero tyres of the correct size. The 20in wheels necessitated the fitting of rubberised rear wheelarch extensions to meet the construction and use regulations criteria.

Also available were much improved brakes based on racing technology. Brembo designed them with two-

The massive 20in Detroit R-Performance wheels, a feature of the XK180 that finally made production on the XKR. (Nigel Thorley)

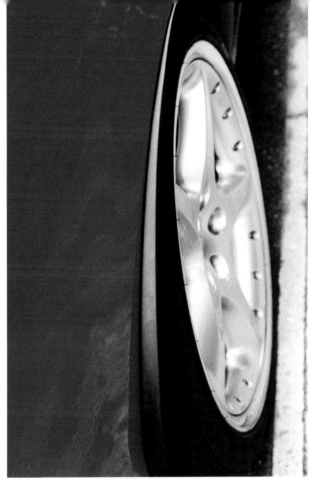

piece, cross-drilled, ventilated discs, 355 x 32mm at the front and 330 x 28mm at the rear, with aluminium four pot callipers bearing the Jaguar name. There was also a Handling Pack, which could only be fitted to cars with CATS suspension. This was made up of your choice of wheels plus the Brembo brakes, uprated springs, anti-roll bars, and retuned variable ratio steering and dampers. With this option ride-height was reduced by 10mm.

Prices for the R-Performance enhancements ranged from £1,450 for the Milan 18in wheels with Pirelli 245/45 and 255/45 tyres, to £5,900 for a fully kitted-out

Rubberised wheelarch extensions are required for the fitment of 20in wheels and tyres to an XK. They are glued and screwed in position. (Nigel Thorley)

Mid-term XKR model with R-Performance Detroit alloy wheels showing the wheelarch extensions and wider track generated by the larger wheels. Note also the removal of the 'Supercharged' boot badge by this time. (Nigel Thorley)

XKR Handling Pack. A full breakdown of the components can be found in the appendices.

1999 Press reviews

Autocar carried out an interesting comparison road test between the XKR – the car they rated as the best front-engined grand tourer – the TVR Cerbera Speed 6, and the Maserati 3200 GT, a very close and new rival to the Jaguar. From the appearance standpoint they still commented on the XKR's high stance with loads of space between wheels and arches and the enormous rear overhang. The Maserati was commended for its uniqueness and purposeful style while the very low, long TVR wouldn't win any awards but was instantly identifiable, more so than the Maserati.

Internally they found the Maserati the most comfortable and roomy, with many Fiat 'hand-me-downs', the Jaguar cramped with fussy instruments, and the TVR claustrophobic and over-stylised. In contrast, the XKR was mechanically the smoothest and deceptively fast because of its cosseted feel and behaviour. The Maserati was harsh and difficult to control and had a heavy clutch, and the TVR, with an even heavier clutch, was noisy and uncomfortable for long-legged drivers, and had a longwinded gear change and over-light throttle.

In conclusion they decided the Jaguar was, overall, the best of the three but in need of better brakes, a larger fuel tank, and more space inside. The Maserati could have won the contest but lacked development in its dynamics, and the TVR was just a raw basic sports car for a specialised market.

When evaluating the relevant costs and benefits of owning a £35,000 used sports car with 2+2 seating in mid-1999, there seemed a clear choice between a 1996 P-registered XK8 Coupé, a 1995 M-registered Porsche 928 GTS, or a 1997 P-registered BMW 840Ci. *Autocar* considered the XK8 was let down by its interior. The BMW was old and had a cramped cabin area but had superb build quality, while the aged Porsche offered rock-steady reliability, performance, and top resale values. However, could either the Porsche or BMW offer the street cred of the Jaguar?

Another *Autocar* road test appeared in October 1999, this time featuring an XKR Convertible with the latest R-Performance additions. Tested at an all-in price of £66,000, the car had the total Handling Pack with big brakes, and uprated and lowered suspension. *Autocar* still waxed lyrical about the car's long-legged cruising ability and mid-range overtaking capabilities but were even keener to write about the improved braking system. It apparently took the tester five consecutive full-bore stops from 130mph to induce any brake fade, and stopping the car from 70mph required two metres less space than the standard XKR. They also identified far better feel from the brakes under all conditions.

Unfortunately they didn't have the same opinion of the handling. Despite the SVO improvements the steering still let the car down and the handling was not up to the standard expected from drivers of Porsche 911s and the like. Body control was noticeably tauter and the bigger tyres and wheels and stiffened suspension didn't have too adverse an affect on the ride, which improved with speed. They concluded that the additions had done an excellent job but that the Jaguar still needed more, and many would have argued that the extra £6,000 the R-Performance options cost should have been on the car from the start, as an inclusive package.

Chapter Six

The millennium and beyond

2000 model year changes

For the 2000 model year Jaguar had to keep abreast of increasing competition and newer and more sophisticated technology. So first off they provided the XK with the Adaptive Cruise Control system (developed for Jaguar by Delphi Automotive Systems), which later became a standard fitment on XKR models and optional on XK8s. This has at its heart a microwave sensor about the size of a shoebox and weighing 1kg, which is mounted in the nose section and acts as a detector system, monitoring what lies ahead of the car by means of a radar aerial and proximity sensor, and relating the information to control units for the engine, transmission and brakes. It is activated by a button alongside the Sport-mode button on the centre console, with a readout in the speedometer.

Activating the console button allows settings to be made via push-buttons on the steering wheel: you set the speed the car is to maintain (exactly the same as with a conventional cruise control, except that you can control it by 1mph increments indicated on the speedometer readout), and then set the trailing distance you wish to maintain from the vehicle in front. Once on the move, you select 'cruise' and the car does the rest. It detects moving traffic and carries out a mathematical evaluation compared to the car's speed and makes the appropriate adjustments smoothly and in plenty of time, dependent on the speed differential. If the vehicle in front turns off or moves into another lane, the system identifies this and increases the speed accordingly back to the pre-set cruise figure. Alternatively, if the vehicle in front continues to slow, perhaps for a junction or hazard, the ACC continues to recalculate the necessary action. It does not, however, take regard of stationary objects, nor will it bring the

car completely to a halt. At a safe distance it sounds a warning, coupled with an indication in the speedometer display that the driver must take control.

Next, although satellite navigation had been around for a few years – and, indeed, Jaguar had introduced a CD system for their S-type in 1999 – it wasn't until 2000 that the XK sports models became available with a fully integrated system. This was a much faster DVD based system which integrated well into the car, with the appropriate equipment in the boot and the colour screen situated in the centre dash area below the air conditioning vents, occupying the space usually taken by the auxiliary gauges. The analogue clock also

The integrated satnav system replaced the auxiliary gauges in the centre of the dashboard. A clear display, concise and easy to understand controls and clear voicing made it a very good DVD-based system. The only downside to the original design was the small digital clock in the bottom left corner, later changed. (Nigel Thorley)

disappeared, being replaced initially by a small digital readout on the satnav screen.

Rain-sensing wipers became a standard fitment on all XK8 models the same year, controlled via the usual steering-column mounted stalk in the 'auto' position. At the same time the anti-lock braking systems were upgraded with 'ABS Plus', designed to recognise the difference in wheel speed and distribute brake pressure accordingly during high-speed braking.

The normal audio system was upgraded with six speakers, and the CD six-disc autochanger became standard equipment on all models. The Premium sound system was also changed to a more impressive Alpine unit providing 320 watts of power, compared to 80 watts from the old system. The Alpine unit also allowed independent adjustment of the sub-woofer bass speaker.

It should also be mentioned at this point that, for the 2000 model year, Jaguar redesigned the engine to accommodate conventional steel cylinder bore liners which, although increasing the weight, eliminated the embarrassing problem of the Nikasil lining wearing away and leading to premature failure of the engine. Further information on this aspect of pre-2000 cars can be found in chapters 8 and 9.

With the above changes Jaguar had improved the value-for-money aspect of the XK range. With no price increases in 2002 they would, in fact, add around £4,900 of value.

Competition in 2000

Though Lexus – who had long been a threat not only to Jaguar but also to Mercedes and BMW – lacked a degree of street cred, they were busily working on improving this in 2000 with a concept car (later to go into production), the Sports Coupé. As Toyota put it at the time, this was strategically aimed at customers who purchased cars like the Jaguar XK8. Strictly a 2+2 of similar proportions to the Jaguar, they even tried to emulate the Spitfire-style dashboard of the XK. But the big advantage came from its fully-retractable metal roof, which folded away into the boot à la Mercedes SLK, although it left no room for luggage when down!

The year 2000 saw an interesting development in the second-hand market for XK8s. After a period of alarming price mark-downs by the trade and a so-called 'glut' of used cars for sale, things changed for the better. An upsurge occurred in the demand for prestige coupés and convertibles, and the XKs benefited from it. Strong demand from customers who were realising the value-for-money of used XKs, compared to the likes of Astons, Porsches and Ferraris, actually forced prices up, and Jaguar dealers in particular were very keen to acquire good low-mileage examples at above 'book' price. Strangely, though, the right specification was still vital to a good sale, the car ideally needing 18in wheels, the right colour, and Classic trim.

It was a testament to where Jaguar had got to in improving their build quality and reputation – nothing like this could have been said for the likes of the XJ-S, the E-type, or even the XK120 after a few years in production.

The F-type unveiled

Mention was made in the previous chapter about the strong possibility of a smaller version of the XK, perhaps an XK6, based on the mid-sized S-type platform. Those rumours turned into reality at the Detroit International Auto Show in January 2000, when Jaguar gave the world its first sighting of the F-type Concept (coded X-600), the spiritual successor to the E-type and more of a true sports car than the XK8.

Ever since announcing the XK180 Jaguar had been debating the possibility of another sporting car to their line-up, in addition to, rather than instead of, the XK8. Meetings had been held with Ford in the US and focus groups had been organised with the owners of rival cars like the BMW Z3, Porsche Boxster and Mercedes SLK. The feedback was so positive that Jaguar and Ford were encouraged to commence work on the X-600.

Given another clean sheet of paper, Keith Helfet (who was behind the XK180) was given free reign to produce the F-type 'in the flesh', from which Jaguar could gauge public reaction in a different marketing environment to that currently satisfied by the XK. The final result owed nothing to existing Jaguar or Ford floorpans but was unique, which, in itself, presented problems for those who had to work on the feasibility of turning the

If the XK180 concept car was pretty, then the F-type was positively beautiful. Extremely well proportioned with an ease of line and compact dimensions – everything a Jaguar sports car should be and an ideal little sister to the XK. (Nigel Thorley collection)

The F-type's lines showed off to their best advantage, perhaps. The family connection with the XK180 can be clearly seen. (Nigel Thorley collection)

The F-type's interior bore a very close resemblance to the XK180:
alloy dashes are back in fashion. (Nigel Thorley collection)

concept into a production vehicle. The concept had no
weather protection, and didn't have a tall enough
windscreen or proper side windows to provide
protection from the wind and other elements. Nor was
it a runner, so adaptations would need to be made to
allow for the engine. And as for that inevitable floorpan
– if bespoke, it could cost millions, if used from the
existing S-type or the still-to-be-announced X-type
smaller saloon, that might compromise the purity of
the original concept design.

The reader might therefore consider that the F-type
Concept bears no resemblance to, nor need be of any
concern to devotees of, the XK8 and XKR, but that
would be a little unfair. The F-type would have ridden
on the back of XK's success and would undoubtedly
have become the offspring of the bigger car. The
anticipated style would have echoed, in many respects,
that of the XK, and despite initial comments it would
have to have shared some items from its parts bin to be
economically viable. Had it been produced, the F-type
Concept would have been significantly smaller than the
XK (25in shorter and 4in narrower), would have been
strictly a two-seater, and would have cost around
£30–35,000.

Subsequently the F-type Concept became the subject
of a detailed 12-month feasibility study at Jaguar and
Ford, and this, plus the overwhelmingly positive public
reaction to the car, convinced them to give the go-
ahead. An official announcement was made at the Los
Angeles International Auto Show in January 2001 that it
was 'go', and that it would take about three years to
bring the F-type Roadster to production 'to
complement the XK range'.

Despite its dealerships accepting deposits in
advance of seeing an actual car, bad news followed in
2002 when Jaguar announced that it was shelving the
F-type project as a result of being overstretched with
work on existing models such as the S-type, the X-
type, and the then still to come Diesel development
and the alloy XJ.

I personally remember visiting Jaguar's Public Affairs
Department and being shown an A4 ring-binder stuffed
full of complimentary comments, letters and even
offers to buy the F-type, and indeed many Jaguar
dealerships reported having extensive lists of
customers' names in readiness for an official order
book. Its cancellation was a sad day, which left the
mantle of Jaguar sporting models with the XK8.

Silverstone special edition

In April 2000, in time for the British Grand Prix at
Silverstone and coinciding with their commitment to
Formula One racing, Jaguar announced the launch of a
special edition XKR, appropriately called the
Silverstone. Just 100 examples were to be sold, 50 as
Coupés and 50 as Convertibles, all of which would be
finished in Platinum Silver exterior finish with a black

hood on the Convertibles. The only external difference to standard XKRs was the unique bonnet and boot badges carrying the words 'Jaguar Silverstone', with the growler image on a black background with grey surround.

Silverstones were fitted as standard with the 20in Detroit split-rim R-Performance alloy wheels, with matching Pirelli P-Zero ultra low profile tyres. The Coupés were further enhanced with the R-Performance Handling Package with bigger brakes, uprated anti-roll bars and springs, and recalibrated steering and dampers. Internally the sill tread plates also carried the 'Silverstone' inscription, and all the cars were trimmed with Sports seats in Warm Charcoal (black) leather with red stitching, matched to similar carpeting and a leather sports steering wheel. The woodwork chosen for all these special editions was grey smoke-stained birds eye maple with the 'Silverstone' insignia laser-etched on the passenger side. As befitted the high standard specification of these cars, they were also equipped with the Jaguar Alpine Premium Sound System with stacker CD system in the boot. Prices for the Silverstone models were: XKR Coupé £66,785, XKR Convertible £72,185.

2001 and more updates

For the 2001 model year Jaguar made a number of changes to the XK range which, in the main, tidied up the look of the car and enhanced the specification. This was managed without any price increases at all at the time – in fact there were actual reductions in the XK range. 2001 prices were:

XK8 Coupé	£48,700 (down by 6.5 per cent)
XK8 Convertible	£55,350 (down by 6.3 per cent)
XKR Coupé	£56,700 (down by 7.4 per cent)
XKR Convertible	£63,350 (down by 7.2 per cent)

Starting at the front, the fog lamps were changed to a flush mounted style, with a new bumper to accommodate them. This gave the fog lights more prominence and imparted a cleaner look to the front of the car. The chrome splitter bar on the XK8 model also came in for slight revision.

The only changes to the side view involved the wheels. On XK8 models the original 17in Revolver wheels were replaced by a new 17in Lamina design, while on cars supplied with the CATS suspension package another new wheel, the 18in Impeller, replaced the original 18in Flute wheels. Double Five 18in wheels remained the norm for XKR models, with the option of 19in Apollo wheels, unless R-Performance options were fitted.

Following on from the S-type saloon, at the rear the XK models took advantage of the new 'jewelled' style of

The main frontal difference from 2001 was the revised style and fitting of fog lamps (revised lamp on right), which also affected the nose itself. (Nigel Thorley)

The restyled bumper showed less of the underside and incorporated a clip-on cover concealing the towing hook. Jewelled rear lighting, now surrounded by chrome trim, and an S-type style plinth with push-button operation, were all 2001 XK features. (Nigel Thorley)

rear light units, also sporting chromed surrounds. Much brighter than the old style, the rear wings were subtly altered internally to accommodate the new lighting.

Better news, and long overdue, was the fitment of an external electrically actuating unlocking button to the boot lid. The button, with a growler emblem, was fitted in the centre of a chrome-plated boot plinth above the registration plate embossed with the name 'Jaguar'. Of the same design as used on the S-type saloons, this also incorporated the registration number lighting unit. The conventional key lock within the XK8 badge remained. Another change at the rear was the bumper style, which now had a small under-spoiler that was deeper, to hide more of the boot floor and underside of the car. This also incorporated a hidden cover under which a towing eye was concealed, different to the exposed eye on the earlier cars. Larger chromed exhaust tail-pipes were fitted to XKR models, bringing this car into line with the same treatment given to XJR saloons of the period.

Technology having moved forward for the 2001 model year, all XKs benefited from further safety features like the fitment of side airbags for the first time on XK models and the latest Adaptive Restraint Technology System (ARTS), the first time this was fitted to a car. This system uses an ultrasonic detector to gauge the position of the front passenger, which is linked to other sensors (situated in the A and B posts, the centre console and the seats) to determine the weight of the passenger, the position of the driver in relation to the steering wheel, and whether one or both parties are wearing a seatbelt. Every ten milliseconds the sensors react to determine whether or not and at what level to deploy the airbags in an accident. This means that if there is no passenger in the front seat, the side airbag is not deployed at all, and if someone is in too close proximity to the dashboard or steering wheel, the airbags are deployed at a lesser level, for safety reasons.

Another safety aspect involved modifying the bodyshell to include reinforced front side-members for added rigidity. This had the added benefit of accommodating various sensors required for the ARTS system. At the same time, to meet new legislation child safety restraints were built into the body-in-white.

A change to the fairly new Adaptive Cruise Control (ACC) enabled the set speed on the cruise control to be always displayed in front of the driver. In the event of the radar sensor in the nose becoming blocked with mud and dirt a 'sensor blocked' message now appeared to alert the driver.

The interior too underwent changes at this time, with a major redesign of the seating. With stronger and more pronounced bolsters for better support, the opportunity was taken to revise the style of pleating. For XK8 models the Classic five flutes were used, while the XKRs had a Sports embossed style with horizontal

All-new seating in 2001, the first major interior change since 1996: separate and adjustable head restraints, revised pleat style and thicker seat backs with better adjustment, all at the expense of rear seating accommodation. (Nigel Thorley)

curved pleating, which was an optional extra on XK8s. All XKs, regardless of specification, now came with electric 12-way adjustable front seating, with separate adjustment for height of the front seat cushions/backs and separate, electrically adjustable head restraints. When a front seat back was folded forward for access to the rear compartment, the head restraints automatically retracted to their lowest position, and reverted to their chosen position when the seat back was returned.

Modification of the seatbelts meant that when the buckle was connected, an electrical contact was made which allowed a 'comfort spring' to come into operation, making for a more comfortable seatbelt fit. On Coupé models the seatbelt height adjusters were redesigned to be more ergonomic. A final interior change saw the addition of 'mood lighting', which emits ambient light to the interior of the cockpit at night.

BIRTH CONTROL

In 2001 Jaguar's Director of Communications and Public Affairs, Stuart Dyble, was driving his pregnant wife to hospital in his silver XKR. Within minutes his wife Vanessa had given birth to their new daughter Sophie in the car. So those road testers who may have complained about lack of room – think again!

Dual band telephone systems also became available for the XK in 2001. (Nigel Thorley)

A new extra cost option was the availability of a dual band, fixed in-car telephone system in the XK. This enabled the phone to switch between networks to ensure the best reception with a lesser chance of losing a call. A revised filtering system cut out unwanted background noise, providing better hands-free

Another XK special edition, the XKR 100, of which just 100 were made. (Nigel Thorley collection)

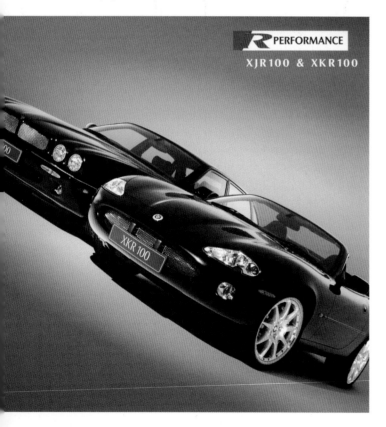

reception. The dual band phone system, although expensive, also incorporated Voice Activation for the dialling of up to 20 pre-programmed telephone numbers.

A data port could also now be fitted to allow information to be transferred to and from a laptop and a memo recording device. As a further accessory an owner could specify a mobile phone charging point, sited inside the glove box.

Up to this time owners of XKs who wanted a reverse park aid fitted had to arrange this with a Jaguar dealer as an after-market fit. From 2001 this could be specified on the original order for a car and fitted during assembly.

Exterior paint schemes changed again, with Spindrift (white) and Alpine (green) being deleted and a standardisation of the colours available on XK8 and XKR models.

Centenary car

Jaguar announced a limited special edition of the XKR in 2001. This was the XKR 100, commemorating the 100th anniversary of the birth of Sir William Lyons, the founder of the company. Just 50 Coupés and 50 Convertibles were produced, all finished in black with matching black leather interior and contrast piping. They were fitted with the R-Performance Handling Pack, alloy surrounds to the instruments and gear lever surround, drilled alloy pedals, special commemorative plaques signifying their uniqueness and, of course unique exterior badging.

Flying the flag

Jaguar prepared a special Union Jack-adorned XK8 Convertible for the Austin Powers movie *Goldmember*. This was also used for promotional purposes in North America when Jaguar announced their 'London Calling' advertising campaign. Subsequently a number of Jaguar dealers 'dressed' other XK8s in the same style for promotional use. The original Austin Powers car is now in the hands of the Jaguar Daimler Heritage Trust.

Production figures

At 14,929 cars 1997 was the peak year of XK production, with a drop in overall numbers to 13,221 in 1998 and 11,421 in 1999. After a slight increase in 2000 to 12,241 production fell again in 2001, to the lowest figure yet for a full year of 10,735.

In the 2001 JD Power survey Jaguar again achieved good results, enjoying a third consecutive year in the top ten for the XJ saloon. The XK sports achieved better results with a fifth place, behind the Audi TT in first, Porsche Boxster second, Porsche 911 third, and Jaguar's own XJ fourth. The XK managed sixth place in the sound system class behind Lexus, BMW and the Jaguar XJ again, and fifth in the best heating and cooling category. It scored consistently high in most categories except for ownership costs, mechanical and exterior problems. The general comments were: 'The JD Power debut reveals real strengths, especially its road ability, cabin assembly and style. However, the cabin is too impractical, seats are prone to faults and bodywork is iffy.'

Press comparisons

The American *Road & Track* magazine had run an XK8 Convertible from 1997 until towards the end of 1999, and after nearly 50,000 miles they rated the car very highly. Apart from a minor accident necessitating the replacement of the front bumper, they got 31,500 miles out of a set of Pirelli tyres. Based on depreciation at that time, taking into consideration the mileage, *Road & Track* estimated that the XK8 had taken a $21,570 'hit' in value, making the price per mile running costs about 89 cents – expensive. Out of pocket maintenance involved replacing the brake discs, a new fog lamp, a

gearshift rubber and, of course, tyres. But they were sorry to see the car go back!

At numerous times the motoring media have compared the XK range with the opposition or even with Jaguar's previous model, the XJS. In 2002 *Jaguar World Monthly* magazine even compared the XK against a choice of two other pre-owned Jaguars and a new X-type 2.0 litre, all offered at similar prices. The choice between a 1997 XK8 Coupé, a 1998 XJR saloon, a 2000 model year S-type and the new X-type seemed automatically to favour the XK8 but, as they pointed out, at that time it was very hard to find an example within this price range and then not necessarily to the specification and colour you might desire. One also had to bear in mind the practicalities of the issue. Though £20,000 may have seemed a reasonable figure and the choice one-sided, was the XK8 the most suitable vehicle for your requirements? This is an argument that still carries weight today, especially when compared to the practicalities and performance of, say, the XJR.

They carried out another comparison at the end of 2004 between a used XK8 and a BMW 840ci, the former

The Austin Powers 'Shaguar', now part of the Jaguar Daimler Heritage Trust collection of vehicles. (Nigel Thorley)

The muscular XKR-R doing what it does best – perform.
(Nigel Thorley)

having the looks, while the latter provided better driver well-being, with firmer suspension and solid build quality.

Full racing seats and harness, Alcantara trim and an adrenalin rush when you rev the engine! (Nigel Thorley)

XKR-R

And now onto the fastest XKR of them all – the XKR-R, a one-off experimental Jaguar that came out of the Special Vehicle Operations Department, which had been responsible for the XK180 and later R-Performance options. The idea was to create the ultimate XKR sports car, stiffer, more agile, and with improved performance and more macho. This is what

Jaguar wanted to compete with the likes of the Mercedes AMG cars and the BMW Alpina.

The project started with a completely conventional XKR Coupé. The whole bodyshell was strengthened to increase stiffness in order to take a different drivetrain. The front end was seam welded for strength, with the front crossbeam solidly mounted with aluminium instead of rubber mounts. The beefed-up steering rack devised for the XK180 was also fitted. At the rear a half roll cage was welded into place replacing the rear +2 seating arrangement of the conventional car, and the rear end of the bodyshell, aft of the floorpan, was cut away and an S-type rear end carefully welded into place.

With these changes carried out, a complete S-type rear suspension/axle assembly was fitted. With technology moving on so fast, even the XK's set-up, derived from the XJ saloon, was not practical for higher performance, the S-type's offering a greater range of ride and handling capabilities.

Competition-style spring and damper units were fitted with individual reservoirs and spherical top mounts, and the whole car was lowered to improve the centre of gravity, becoming 30mm lower than a conventional XK8 and 20mm lower than an XKR. It was fitted with 20in R-Performance split-rim wheels and ultra-low profile tyres. With the added benefit of the then still new revised front and rear bumper treatment, and the addition of straight over-sills (shades of revised production XK still to come), the end product looked aggressive and powerful even when standing still.

Under the bonnet, the engine was still the 4.0-litre AJ-V8 unit, but fitted with twin carbon fibre air intakes. Like the XK180 engine the crankshaft pulley size was increased to raise the boost level and a bigger intercooler and radiator also helped. The end result was an engine achieving up to 450bhp at 6,200 rpm. To push the gases through a massive straight-through exhaust system was hand-crafted, with four tail-pipes.

SVO opted to fit a six-speed manual gearbox, using a Tremec T-56 mated to the engine via a two-plate clutch, as fitted to cars like the Aston Martin Vantage, Chevrolet Corvette and Dodge Viper. Finally, the handbrake was an electrical/hydraulic system operated from a rather elongated handle by the driver's seat.

Internally, all the wood veneer was replaced by carbon fibre, new to the XK at that time. Alcantara was used for some of the trim, along with racing-style Recaro seating with full harnesses – no shopping car this!

This one-off car is now in the hands of the Jaguar Daimler Heritage Trust and although never put into

Over 450bhp from the modified 4.0-litre engine fitted to the XKR-R. (Nigel Thorley)

production for cost reasons, elements subsequently found their way through to production XKs and also to the new aluminium XK replacement.

The 2001 model year XKR Convertible finished in Platinum Silver with 18in Double Five wheels. (Nigel Thorley)

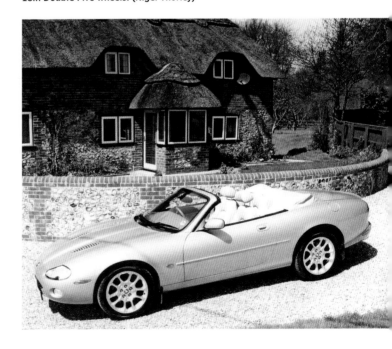

The new generation XK

Falling sales

Although, as a company, Jaguar was doing quite nicely, the XK wasn't doing so well. From a production high of nearly 15,000 cars in 1997 sales had deteriorated to under 11,000 by 2001, and got dramatically worse from there on. The total production figure for 2002 was a mere 6,861 cars, and that reflected in sales, as it was now pretty easy to find new XKs in the dealer showrooms awaiting customers.

This should, of course, be put into context, as after being Jaguar's bestselling sports car ever it was inevitable that after six years sales would drop, and even then they remained favourable compared to some of the later XJS models. Another 'hit' on XK sales may well have been the publication by the motoring press of 'spy' photographs of what was supposedly the next new XK, but was in reality no more than a revamp of the existing model.

Jaguar therefore needed to revitalise interest in the XK, and more changes took place for the last phase in its lifespan.

A new, highly sophisticated six-speed gearbox, later standardised for all XK models. (Nigel Thorley collection)

Six-speeder

Late in 1999 ZF announced the forthcoming introduction of their first six-speed automatic transmission, Model No 6HP 26, specifically designed for rear-wheel drive performance cars. This was to eventually replace the ZF 5HP 24 five-speed unit used in the normally aspirated XK8 models and the Mercedes W5A 580 box in the XKR cars.

The big advantage, apart from more gears, was that with improved technology the new gearbox was 12 per cent lighter and 50mm shorter than the old five-speed unit, but with a greater torque capability. Although a die-cast casing, the new gearbox used a glass-reinforced plastic sump to keep weight down. It also incorporated a new Bosch TCM (Transmission Control Module) integrated into the main gearbox housing with cable and plug connections. The use of six gears provided a wider spread of ratios and, of course, a taller top (sixth) gear which ZF claimed would result in improvements of between 1 and 5 per cent in acceleration and 5 to 7 per cent in fuel economy.

Another innovation with the new gearbox was a torque converter that cut off at idle so that the engine wasn't under load when the car was stationary. ZF also integrated the 'mechatronic' electronic module into the gearbox housing to improve the quality of gear shifts.

This new gearbox was produced in 2001, when Jaguar became one of the first customers to use it, though at that time only on the S-type mid-range saloon. But its use in the XK soon followed.

2002 changes

New Jaguar buyers (of any model) benefited from a revised policy on new car warranties. From now on all new Jaguars (including XKs) received a comprehensive three-year, unlimited mileage warranty (previously 60,000 miles). This had a two-fold effect on the reputation of the company and its cars. Firstly it only came about from the fact that Jaguar had improved its build quality and longevity significantly in recent years; and secondly it sent out important signals to those contemplating buying a Jaguar.

More importantly, however, big changes were in hand for the 2003 model year XK range. Dubbed by the company 'The New-Generation Jaguar XK', these were to be the most significant changes to the model range since its introduction in 1996. They revolved around an

Jaguar's new 4.2-litre engine for the 2003 model year, codenamed AJ-34. (Nigel Thorley collection)

enlarged engine, the new gearbox, better brakes and chassis, improved electronics and revised trim. At the heart of these changes was the adoption of a new version of the AJ-V8 engine (coded AJ-34), enlarged to 4.2 litres (4,196cc) capacity, first seen in S-type saloons. The logic behind the redesign was to improve performance and economy.

Many internal changes took place and the whole engine was claimed to be stiffer than the version it replaced. Indeed, the pistons, for example, were forged from single billets of aluminium and had jet cooling on the underside of the crowns. The new engine also benefited from variable camshaft phasing, in which an hydraulic actuator on each inlet camshaft is operated by a pair of electronically-switched oil pressure control valves, actuated by the engine control module, which contains maps of engine speeds and loads. This produces faster engine response and optimum performance at all engine speeds, which in turn helps emissions. The induction system was also amended with multi-hole injectors to refine the spray pattern in the combustion chamber, and the block and bed-plate were redesigned for extra lightness (6kg lighter than the outgoing 4.0-litre).

For the supercharged installation, an Eaton unit was again fitted, with an industry first on a production car: helical rotor gears for low noise. The supercharger

From 2003 on XKs received new badging, in the XKR's case directly from R-Performance. Similarly, the higher performance models got their rear plinth finished in body colour. (Nigel Thorley collection)

Adopting the ZF 6HP 26 six-speed automatic transmission for all XKs at the same time as the introduction of the new engine eliminated the necessity for two different gearboxes. A final change in the drive train involved a revised rear axle ratio to suit the new gearbox and the increased torque of the engine.

Engine comparisons

	4.0 litre	4.0 litre s/c	4.2 litre	4.2 litre s/c
Engine capacity (cc)	3,996	3,996	4,196	4,196
Bore x stroke (mm)	86 x 86	86 x 86	86 x 90.3	86 x 90.3
Maximum power (bhp @ revs)	290 @ 6,100	370 @ 6,150	300 @ 6,000	400 @ 6,100
Maximum torque (lb ft @ revs)	290 @ 6,100	387 @ 3,600	310 @ 4,100	408 @ 3,500
Compression ratio	10.75:1	9.0:1	11.0:1	9.1:1
Top speed (limited)	155mph	155mph	155mph	155mph
0–60mph (seconds)	6.7	5.3	6.1	5.3
Av fuel consumption (mpg)	23.9	22.6	24.9	22.6

therefore spins 5 per cent faster than the one used in the 4.0-litre engine.

In the XK8 installation the new engine produced 300bhp at 6,000rpm in standard form. Fitted to the XKR model with supercharger, it boasted 400bhp and significantly improved torque up to 408lb ft. Compared to previous models, the 4.2-litre engine improved performance all round by 3½ per cent in the XK8 and 8 per cent in the XKR. Jaguar claimed not only better performance but also improved refinement and fuel economy, as demonstrated by the figures given here.

2003 car with the then new standard equipment Gemini 17in alloy wheels for the XK8. (Nigel Thorley)

With improved performance came improved brakes, the Brembo now being adopted with larger ventilated discs (355mm x 32mm front and 330mm x 28mm rear), four pot callipers and steel braided flexible brake lines as standard on XKR models. Non-supercharged models had the enlarged standard discs (325mm x 28mm front and 305mm x 20mm rear). Another standard fit on all models was the new EBA (Emergency Brake Assist)

technology, which automatically applies additional braking pressure if the driver has not provided it under extreme conditions.

The Adaptive Restraint Technology mentioned earlier also became standard equipment on all XK models. CATS suspension remained a standard fit on XKR models but was an extra cost option on XK8s. Yet more standard fit features on all models were DSC (Dynamic Stability Control) and cruise control.

Externally the changes for the 2003 model year were more subtle. Following Jaguar practice with all its other models, new rear badging was of a cleaner style and the R-Performance logo was adopted for XKR models. The boot finisher above the number plate was from then on body-coloured for XKR models.

Front light units changed, all cars featuring black surround recesses to the headlamp units, with Xenon gas headlights standard on XKR models along with automated headlamp levelling. An 'Autolamp' mode was added, to automatically switch them on in poor ambient light. Also, within 20 seconds of turning the wipers on the lights would also switch on.

More alloy wheel changes also took place at this time. Gemini 17in became the standard fitment on XK8 cars, while two new 18in styles – Hydra and Centaur – became available for the XKR and optional at extra cost on the XK8. With these additions Jaguar offered a comprehensive range of alloy wheels from the base 17in size up to R-Performance split-rim 20in.

The final external change came in the range of paint finishes. New paint schemes were Adriatic Blue (metallic mid-blue), displacing Sapphire; Jaguar Racing Green (darker metallic green with lighter under-tones); Ebony (solid black); and Midnight (Metallic black), displacing Anthracite. Other displaced colours were Emerald Green, Platinum Grey, Mistral Blue, Roman Bronze, Titanium Grey, and Westminster Blue. As can be seen, the total range of exterior colours was thus dramatically reduced.

Internally a new style leather and alloy gear-knob featured on XKR models, all dashboards now featured an etched leaping cat emblem on the passenger airbag door, and there were quite dramatic changes in the trim style and colour schemes. The choice now included themes first seen in the small X-type saloons of single or even dual colour options, like Heritage Tan with Warm Charcoal and Cranberry with Warm Charcoal. For the traditional finishes, Dove Grey was added to the popular Cashmere and Ivory.

In addition there was the option of having factory-fitted Recaro sports seating trimmed in soft grain leather in a choice of three colours, plus an aluminium pack based on instrument bezel and J-gate surrounds, door release levers, pedal pads and sill tread plates (standard on XKR models). The instruments were amended on all models anyway, with a new domed style of finisher.

New accessories for all XK models at this time included an electronic compass display within the self-dimming electrochromatic interior rear view mirror and a DVD-based satnav system with additional country coverage in Spain, Portugal, Sweden and Denmark. A digitally generated analogue clock could now be displayed in the navigational screen as well. The previously discussed ACC (Adaptive Cruise Control) could now be fitted to XK8 models as well as the XKR.

Prices were raised for the 2003 model year to the following:

XK8 Coupé	£48,700	$69,995
XK8 Convertible	£55,350	$74,995
XKR Coupé	£56,700	$81,995
XKR Convertible	£63,350	$86,995

Jaguar made a slight stylistic change to all XKs a few months later when the exterior side rubbing strips were removed to clean up the line of the car.

The competition

Jaguar XK sales were still tailing off, with a total production figure of just 5,656 in 2003. This was nearly 18 per cent down on the previous year and the trend looked likely to continue in 2004. Despite all the upgrades, improvements and enhancements, the XK, although still looking the part, was falling behind the competition in many ways.

For example, the Mercedes SL looked more contemporary than the XK, and their AMG-modified SL550 showed the company's commitment to enhanced versions of standard production cars. TVR had their new T350 Coupé along with other models

2003 model year XKR Convertible in Platinum Silver with xenon headlights and 18in Hydra alloy wheels. (Nigel Thorley collection)

offering sheer grunt and an incredible presence in style and sound, if less refinement than the Jaguar. Chrysler's Crossfire had been joined by a very attractive, and much cheaper, full Convertible model, and Lexus were now promoting their new SC430 Convertible, a very creditable combination of legendary Lexus quality with a sporty and economical 3.2-litre V6 engine, for less money than the equivalent XK Convertible.

Some attractive proper four-seater coupés were also stealing the limelight, including the Mercedes CLK, which with its 5.0-litre V8 engine and full spec came in well below the price of a Jaguar XK8. Oh yes, and the Maserati Spyder (and Coupé) were by now much improved. And let's not forget Porsche, who were offering an incredible 15 sports cars in their range and were still the benchmark by which other manufacturers, even Jaguar, were judged. And lastly, just around the corner was the new BMW 6 Series.

Another special edition

With sales tailing off in the valued United States market Jaguar decided to broaden their appeal with another limited edition car, specifically for that market. Called the Portfolio and only available with the supercharged engine and in Convertible form, it boasted unique colour schemes and interior trim and production was limited to just 200 cars.

The unique exterior paint finishes of blue or red were echoed by matching Boxmark leather centre panels in the seating, door trims, and even the steering wheel, all in the same colours. The seats were of special Recaro

US Portfolio special edition, this one finished in Coronado Blue. Note the lack of side rubbing strip applicable to all later XKs, and the chromed door handles, a standard feature on US models. (Nigel Thorley collection)

Typical uniquely finished interior of the US Portfolio model. (Nigel Thorley collection)

design with integrated headrests. The cars were also treated to 20in Detroit R-Performance wheels and tyres as standard equipment. One hundred examples were

A deeper mouth and new splitter bar at the front for the 2004/2005 XK. (Nigel Thorley)

And the new treatment for the XKR model. (Nigel Thorley collection)

built in Jupiter Red and the other hundred in Coronado Blue, all with a black Convertible roof. All sold in 2004 at a price of $93,995 ($6,000 more than a conventional XKR Convertible).

The last chance Coupé and Convertible

Another year went by and Jaguar was experiencing unequalled growth in new car sales around the world, but this was down to the other models in the range, particularly diesels. In order to maintain that edge they therefore needed to keep the XK competitive on the street for just a little longer. The XK therefore received yet another upgrade, this time more cosmetic than technology-based.

Building on all the changes and updates made over the years, the exterior styling came in for the most significant alterations for this last revamp. In Jaguar's own words, this was to give the car a more contemporary feel. The front got a revised nose section with a deeper mouth for the front air intake and a lower front, which gave the car a more aggressive stance. Jaguar also claimed a performance benefit, as the lower front end improved the aerodynamics. The enlarged mouth necessitated a change in the design of the 'over-riders', the chromed splitter bar and even the number plate mounting on the normally aspirated cars, and a new mesh grille on the XKR models.

To complement the new nose, additional sill covers lowered the sides of the car to match the front and were completely flat in section, 'hiding' the previous sculpted nature of the sill shaping, while at the rear a new bumper and boot spoiler gave the car a slightly more squat appearance. Enlarged exhaust tailpipe trims were used on XK8 models, and a larger rear spoiler and quad tailpipe exhaust finishers on the XKR.

More new wheels completed the external update, with three new multi-spoke options becoming available – the 18in Aris, 19in Atlas, and 20in BBS Sepang – alongside the carryover designs from the previous update, comprising the 17in Gemini (still standard fitment on XK8 models), 18in Hydra (standard on XKRs), and 20in BBS Montreal and Detroit R-performance wheels.

The main body structure and exterior panelling remained unchanged, but the new 'treatment' certainly changed the way the car looked. There were also changes to the choice of exterior paint finishes. A solid black, Ebony, joined the existing Midnight metallic black; Quartz was an additional metallic grey; Radiance and Salza replaced Carnival red; and Ultraviolet (metallic purple) and Zircon (pale metallic blue) were further additions to the range. Black window surrounds were now used on all models, replacing the previous Dorchester grey colour.

Interior alterations

The interior was also refreshed, with the introduction of two new wood veneers. Elm – a lighter hue than the traditional burr walnut – was supposedly a more modern alternative to walnut (which was still offered),

Side view of the 2004/2005 XK8 Coupé, in this instance finished in Zircon Blue and sporting 18in Aris wheels. The revised shaping to the front nose section and rear bumper, along with the 'clip-on' sill covers, clearly differentiate this model from previous XKs. (Nigel Thorley)

while an entirely new finish was Piano Black, a very high-gloss black provided as a no-cost option for XKR customers. The grey stained birds eye maple finish also

The only slightly revised exterior rear view of the later XK8. Note particularly the larger exhaust tailpipes. (Nigel Thorley)

Jaguar's later Piano Black interior treatment for XKs. (Nigel Thorley collection)

ASL is activated by the button that replaces the normal Cruise Control. (Nigel Thorley)

remained available as the standard finish on all models.

An R-Performance option of aluminium surrounds for the facia instrumentation, J-gate gear selector and pedals could now be chosen for an ultra-modern appearance when ordering a car new. The number of interior trim finishes was reduced, and out went the

two-tone finishes described at the beginning of this chapter.

The 2004 Jaguar XK also introduced, as standard, a further key electronics feature in the form of ASL, or Automatic Speed Limiter, standard on all models. The ASL system enhances the security of drivers and passengers by preventing the car from exceeding a pre-

Birds eye maple veneer in an XKR with Recaro seating. (Nigel Thorley collection)

The speed set is shown in the speedometer in front of the driver. (Nigel Thorley)

selected maximum speed. When the driver has programmed a speed beyond which they don't wish to exceed, the Automatic Speed Limiter will constantly monitor the throttle inputs and engine speeds. Once the selected maximum speed is reached, ASL will maintain it even if the throttle pedal is depressed beyond that point. However, to ensure absolute safety, ASL is automatically cancelled if the driver applies full kickdown via the throttle pedal and the automatic transmission. This new feature is operated by a switch on the gearshift surround and steering wheel, and has a readout display on the speedometer.

Special option packs

Coinciding with the introduction of these latest XKs, Jaguar announced a range of what they called 'value for money option packs', which were available in all markets except Japan and North America. There were three packs to choose from: separate Premium Packs for both XK8 and XKR, and a single Technology Pack for both, the object of which was to upgrade their specification significantly.

The XK8 Premium Pack comprised 18in Aris or 19in Atlas wheels; reverse park radar control; heated front windscreen; aluminium J-gate and bezel surrounds; elm wood veneer; sports seats; Xenon headlights; heated mirrors; a seat and mirror positioning memory pack; and cup holders. The XKR Premium Pack comprised 19in Atlas or 20in BBXS wheels; reverse park radar control; heated front windscreen; Recaro seats; cross-drilled brake discs; sports steering wheel and Momo gear-knob; seat positioning memory pack; aluminium J-gate and bezel surrounds; Piano Black veneer (with Burr walnut veneer also optional); and cup holders. Both these packs were also available with a reduced number of items for other world markets (but still not Japan and North America). The Technology Pack comprised Adaptive Cruise Control, Premium sound system, and satellite navigation.

The 'new' XKs went on sale in March 2004 at the following prices:

XK8 Coupé	£49,920 (£49,995 from August 2005)
XK8 Convertible	£56,720 (£56,795 from August 2005)
XKR Coupé	£58,120 (£59,995 from August 2005)
XKR Convertible	£64,920 (£66,795 from August 2005)

Despite falling sales, in September 2004 Jaguar announced that they had sold their 40,000th XK in the States, their most important market. The XK was still the company's most successful sports car ever, despite its production in 2004 reaching only 4,413, an all-time low. However, Jaguar stated that sales of XKs were apparently 30 per cent up on the same period in 2003, which proves that the 'new' models must have had some effect overall.

Introducing carbon fibre

Jaguar were by now quite used to presenting special edition XKs, and late in 2004 another was to appear, this time – initially, at least – exclusively for the UK: the Carbon Fibre car. Just 100 were produced, marketed as the most well equipped XK to date. Based on the XKR and available in either Coupé or Convertible form, this special edition even got a unique and comprehensive full colour brochure of its own, complete with a mock carbon fibre sleeve. The 100 lucky buyers not only got a unique, extremely well equipped car but also got a short-break holiday in either Scotland or Dartmoor, paid for by Jaguar.

It is easier to list what Carbon Fibre models did *not* include as standard features, but items it did come with included, for example, an integrated compass in the rear view mirror, a dual band telephone, a first aid kit and a warning triangle. Buyers could choose any colour they liked from the existing XK range and the same for trim, but – obviously, to match the name of the model – all came with a carbon fibre finished dashboard instead of conventional veneer. What price such opulence? £64,650 for the Coupé and £71,450 for the Convertible, or in the latter case over £4,500 more than an equivalent 'standard' XKR Convertible.

As it turned out another 200 Carbon Fibre cars were subsequently produced and sold into the US market to commemorate Trans-Am racing successes (see later). Slightly different to the UK car, the owners didn't get the option of a weekend break and the seats were fitted with Alcantara inserts and matching door panels.

STILL HALE

The Jaguar XK was still in the running as far as many were concerned, despite being eight years old at the end of 2004, when the Spanish car magazine *Sabre Ruedas* voted the XKR Convertible the best Convertible of the Year. A jury of 15 automotive experts called it 'a true milestone in automotive design'.

Carbon Fibre by name, carbon fibre by trim – the telltale of one of these special edition cars is the unique dash treatment. (Nigel Thorley)

2005 V for Victory and S for Superb

At the NAIAS Motor show in Detroit on 10 January 2005, Jaguar unveiled their stunning new sports car concept, the ALC (Advanced Lightweight Coupé), a car that would

Victory and S models shown in two of their special colour schemes – Satin Silver and Bay Blue. (Nigel Thorley collection)

form the basis of the replacement for the XK8 and XKR, due to be phased out of production that year. This was followed by the announcement at the Geneva Motor Show in March of a European Special Edition XK called the 4.2 S, available in both Coupé and Convertible form with upgrades; and the announcement at the Los Angeles Auto Show in June of the Victory special edition for the US market, supposedly built to celebrate the four Trans-Am championship wins by Rocketsports, who campaigned XKRs.

Available in both XK8 and XKR variants, the Victory had quite a production run, 1,050 cars being manufactured in Coupé and Convertible form. Though it was actually no more than a rebadged 4.2 S, it constituted the last XK model prior to the latter's deletion from the Jaguar range. The only differences

Last of the line, in this case a 4.2 S model with Elm wood veneer. (Nigel Thorley collection)

US Victory model with carbon fibre dash. (Nigel Thorley collection)

Final badging style, which applied to both the 4.2 S and Victory models. (Nigel Thorley collection)

Detail carpet treatment for the 4.2 S and Victory models. (Nigel Thorley collection)

between the Victory and the 4.2 S are the Victory badges and insignia on its sill tread plates: all the other information given below applies to both models.

US Victory model in Copper Black with chromed alloys. (Nigel Thorley collection)

Mechanically these cars were standard, up to the latest specification announced the previous year. Externally they are identifiable by the revised badging on the boot and the growler badges incorporating a chequered flag emblem. Standard wheel fit was the 19in Atlas for the XK8 (the largest standard fit wheels

New badging for the final European models. (Nigel Thorley)

ever offered on an XK8) and 20in split-rim BBS Perseus for the XKR. Although buyers could specify any of the existing Jaguar exterior paint finishes for the 4.2 S, four unique colour schemes were also offered – Copper Black Metallic, Front Blue Metallic, Bay Blue Metallic, and Satin Silver Metallic. Darkened rear light clusters were fitted to all models.

Internally, upon opening the doors the first recognisable change came with the sill tread plate design, highly polished with the chequered flag emblem either side of the model identification. Dash and allied trim areas were finished in Elm on the XK8 or Carbon Fibre on the XKR (with the no extra cost option of Elm), in both cases with alloy edging to the instruments as standard. As well as the standard range of interior trim finishes a new Dove carpet colour was provided for the 4.2 S, with standard fit 'Jaguar' embossed leather edged over-carpets.

Soft grain leather seating was used on all these cars and other, normally extra-cost fitments – like power fold-back mirrors, headlamp power-wash, heated

New badging for the final European models. (Nigel Thorley)

front windscreen, rain sensing wipers, heated seats, Xenon headlamps and Bluetooth connectivity – were standard on both the XK8 and XKR versions. A 320 watt, eight-speaker Premium sound system was also standard equipment. Prices for the XK 4.2 S models were:

XK8 Coupé	£50,477
XK8 Convertible	£57,995
XKR Coupé	£59,995
XKR Convertible	£66,795

So lavish was the price and specification for these cars that Jaguar produced a very attractive and unique hardbound brochure for the car, as a fitting tribute to what would be the last XK8 and XKR produced.

Last variant of the XK8, the 4.2 S in Convertible form finished in Zircon Blue. (Nigel Thorley collection)

The very last XK off the line, an XKR 4.2 S, now part of the Jaguar Daimler Heritage Trust collection of vehicles. (Nigel Thorley)

Closing comments

Howard Walker from the States passed the following comments in *Jaguar World Monthly* magazine leading up to the demise of the XK. He said: 'I've just been driving one of the last-of-the-last XKR Convertibles and I'd forgotten just how drop-dead gorgeous, just how sensuous-like Catherine Zeta the thing is … And to my eyes the car still looks as sexy as hell … See one cruising the boulevards of Beverly Hills and it will still turn heads. The last XKR to me will always be the coolest cat around.'

Final US prices for the XK models as they finished production were:

XK8 Coupé	$70,495
XK8 Convertible	$75,495
XKR Coupé	$81,995
XKR Convertible	$86,995

These prices exclude the USA's usual $1,000 Gas Guzzler tax.

The very last XK rolled off the production lines at Jaguar's Browns Lane factory on Friday 27 May 2005, the last Coupé being handed over to the Jaguar Daimler Heritage Trust. Final production figures for the XK were:

XK8 Coupé	19,748
XK8 Convertible	46,760
XKR Coupé	9,661
XKR Convertible	13,895
Total	90,064

Chapter Eight

Buying an XK8

If you are considering the purchase of an XK model, reading this book will give you a good grounding in the background and development of the model. You can compare specifications, the changes that took place over the ten years of production, and even check out aspects of maintenance and modification, but you need more. In this chapter I plan to give you guidelines regarding what to look for in these cars, but before we go any further there are some fundamental points to consider.

For ultimate value, an early XK8 Coupé with 17in Revolver wheels and few additional goodies can make an ideal entry into XK ownership. This example is finished in Carnival Red with Oatmeal Classic interior. (Nigel Thorley)

Decide on your budget

This is an important issue and will help you narrow the field when looking for a suitable car. There are ample used-car price guides around, which you should study at the time you intend to purchase. This will help you target a particular range of model years or even the type of car.

When budgeting do not just ascertain what you are willing to spend on your acquisition: go a little further and think about the on-the-road costs. Your age and driving experience will dictate insurance premiums, but you should consider the number of miles you intend to cover a year and not only the general maintenance costs, such as the normal 10,000-mile interval servicing, but also, probably, unplanned major repairs, or even the cost of replacing a set of tyres – all of which can turn out to be somewhat daunting to the uninitiated.

Jaguars are expensive cars when new and therefore deserve good, regular maintenance. Normal 10,000-mile service intervals are not extravagantly pricey, particularly if you use a Jaguar independent specialist as opposed to a franchised dealership, but check out the service schedule data in Appendix D and you will

Accumulated dirt and moisture can cause corrosion between the floorpan and reinforcing plates, leading to swelling and eventually cracking as shown here. If the cracking becomes severe, the work involved in rectification is intensive because of the removal of all the interior trim. (Nigel Thorley)

see that at various intervals these services increase both in man-hours and the work required, which will increase the maintenance costs considerably.

The choice of car

With the car having only been in production for ten years, the choice is quite restricted. Once you decide on a Convertible or Coupé, normally-aspirated XK8 or supercharged XKR, your field is significantly narrowed. Coupés will always come cheaper than equivalent Convertibles, since the latter are very popular (particularly, surprisingly, in the UK). XK8s will also always be cheaper than equivalent supercharged models, so this choice is purely down to you and what you want from the vehicle.

For normal everyday driving the performance from (and economy of) the XK8 is perfectly adequate and you could save a lot of money by opting for this choice. If you want extra performance, 'kick-in-the-back' enjoyment and cachet, and don't mind the slight drawback in economy terms and refinement, then you must go with your heart and choose an XKR.

Similarly, the choice between Convertible and Coupé is down to personal preference. Arguably one could say the Coupé looks the more attractive in exterior style, has marginally better visibility and is less vulnerable than the Convertible, but on a warm summer's day, on an open country road, what could be nicer than to drive around in a superbly smooth XK with the top down?

This also applies to interior finish. The Classic trim with conventional walnut veneer is always a good seller, whereas the earlier Sports style with dark stained maple and high contrast trim finishers is never as popular, so this may dictate a price difference. Specification too will play its part in the price you pay. For example, a car equipped with the Premium sound system and cruise control is going to cost more than one without. Compare the specifications in this book to identify what was and wasn't standard on these models over the ten years. In some cases the after-market cost of fitting an extra is prohibitive – items like cruise control should not be considered a viable option for retro-fitting, for example.

I will cover many of the service aspects and known problems with XKs in the next chapter, and some of these should be borne in mind when buying. A service history is essential, though these days that doesn't necessarily have to have been with a Jaguar franchised

A medium mileage, seven-year-old XK8 that had been supposedly well wax-protected – but peeling back the front wheelarch inner panel reveals the start of corrosion! (Nigel Thorley)

The rear sill lip could almost have been designed to collect debris, which will eventually cause corrosion. It is a simple matter to keep it clean and dry. (Nigel Thorley)

Removing the panel will reveal this, looking back towards the cockpit of the car from the nearside front wheelarch (right-hand drive car). Look at the number of places where damp can fester and eventually cause corrosion if not protected. (Nigel Thorley)

The unsightly weld mark along the visible face of the sill can cause problems if the paint cracks like this. (Nigel Thorley)

dealership as long as you have good solid evidence of the work being regularly done by someone who knows the model well.

Body and trim

XK bodies were well protected, but bear in mind that the earliest cars date from 1996 and without regular attention may well have suffered from corrosion somewhere. The XJS-based floorpan can be particularly vulnerable if damaged in any way – it has been known to crack due to swelling caused by corrosion between the floorpan and reinforcing plates. Areas around the joins between the floorpan and the sills can also cause

Although dealers don't recommend the steam cleaning of engine compartments these days because of the level of electronics used, there is no reason that an engine and ancillaries should not look presentable and clean. Note the semi-matt finish to the suspension turrets at either side of the engine bay signifying the original paint finish on these cars, not to the same high standard as the exterior panels. (Nigel Thorley)

problems. Removing the rubberised inner wheelarch panels from the front will reveal areas that, although originally painted, are prone to ingress of dirt and mud, and corrosion will eventually start here too: these areas are best treated regularly with a wax protective substance.

Whilst looking underneath the car, see if the nose or front cross member or even the radiator may have been damaged by speed bumps. Another important area to check is the rear edge of the sill, where it folds under to join the floorpan in the inner wheelarch area and forms a curved lip which will naturally gather dust and debris thrown up from the rear wheels. This debris in turn collects water and eventually corrosion will start. Cleaning this area out regularly and treating it with wax will prevent long-term damage.

Still looking at the sill area, halfway along (below the door aperture) there is a welded join which can stress, eventually leading to cracking in the paint, particularly on Convertibles. This should be checked and if identified cleaned back to metal and repainted.

Typically, as with any other car, debris can build up in the lips of the wheelarches, so look for this and for rust bubbles appearing where damp has begun to eat into the paintwork. The rear wheelarches themselves are vulnerable, as they carry no protective rubberised panels like the front. Painted black from the factory, this 'ordinary' paint wears off over time revealing little beneath except the scantily applied body colour.

Paintwork generally is very good on these cars. You may notice a slight difference in the colour between the plastic nose section and the metal bonnet – this is normal, but if excessive can mean that one or the other has been repainted. This may not be an issue, as all XKs will at some time suffer from pebble rash across the bonnet caused by debris thrown up from the road or other vehicles skimming across it. This is normal and can only be rectified by stripping the bonnet back to bare metal and respraying. Because of the curved nature of the front and rear and the vulnerability of the bumper and nose facings, look for previous or current damage or even badly stone-chipped lights, all of which can be expensive to repair or replace.

As with all modern cars, the factory painting of Jaguars is carried out in a very different manner than it was years ago. This means that the outer panels are well finished whilst the inner faces may not be finished with a topcoat at all. Interior panels such as the interior of the bonnet or inner wings being nicely gloss finished will therefore indicate a repair/repaint at some time.

Paint chips can also be a problem on the screen surround, a grey painted affair on most models. This seems to collect chips and marks which easily fester into corrosion. It is actually more cost effective to replace the surround rather than to remove it, repaint it and refit it – another, although small, cost to consider when buying.

All XKs were equipped with alloy wheels (see Appendix C), but what was supplied originally may not necessarily be on the car now; changing or updating the wheels is normal practice and is no detriment to the car providing the correct type and style of wheel is fitted to Jaguar specification. You should particularly beware after-market non-Jaguar wheels.

All alloy wheels deteriorate over time either because of minor corrosion from the hot dust off the brake pads or by damage from kerbing. This is particularly important with the larger split-rim R-Performance wheels, as these are very expensive to replace, repair

Check the condition of tyres and wheels and ensure the correct size is on the correct wheel. It is not unknown for front wheels (narrower on most XKs) to be fitted at the rear! The condition of split-rim alloys is particularly important, as they tend to be more vulnerable to kerb damage and more costly to repair. (Nigel Thorley)

being a limited option dependent on the amount of damage. All alloys can be refurbished professionally these days but this is another cost to consider when buying one of these cars.

Similarly, look at the tyres. The majority of XKs were fitted with Pirelli or, latterly, Continental tyres. Other tyres can be fitted, of course, provided they fall within the guidelines of size and profile for the car and wheel used. Uneven wear on the tread will give an indication of poor driving, wear in the steering/suspension of the car, or just lack of regular attention to tyre pressures – all signs of a poorly maintained vehicle. Again, tyres don't come cheap with any XK model.

Finally on tyres, remember that the larger wheels (18in and above) normally have asymmetric tyres fitted, which means you must ensure that the direction of rotation as marked on the tyre wall is followed. Check this out, because if they are incorrectly fitted not only will they be unsafe to drive on at speed but they will also contravene current legislation.

Modena Yellow may not be everyone's idea of an XK colour, but it is not unusual to find XKs in unique colour schemes chosen to suit the original owners. (Nigel Thorley)

Lastly the exterior colour scheme should be mentioned (the full range is given in Appendix E). The specific colour chosen by the original purchaser may not be ideal for second and subsequent owners, and this can affect the price, as contemporary fashion plays a major role in the choice of cars and colour schemes. For example, a white XK curries little favour in the UK but is extremely popular in the States and hot countries like South Africa. Black is a fashion colour, particularly popular in the London and Home Counties area of the UK yet not popular at all in the North of England. Statement colours like Aquamarine are niche market for many, and more mundane finishes like Topaz appear not to be suited to the second-hand market for older XKs. Greens are still considered an unlucky colour by many but most blues are very popular, as is silver these days.

When examining an impending purchase, check that there are two sets of keys *and* key fobs. If not, keys are very expensive to replace, and if one of the fobs doesn't activate the locking and arming system it could be that there is no battery in it. If one of these batteries has to be changed, it must be done within a ten-minute period, otherwise the vital link is lost and it can be very expensive to get reprogrammed.

Interior trim

Internally these cars wear well. The first area to check is the seat facings. Always leather (though some Sport cars have a cloth inset), the driver's seat will say a lot about how the car has been used or abused. Seat coverings are not cheap to repair or replace these days unless you buy a second-hand set from an accident-damaged car (some are available). Many XKs featured lighter-coloured upholstery, which shows marks and stains more than darker colours.

Similarly carpets will damage, particularly on the driver's side, from constant use. Over-mats were always available, so if they were not used it is another sign of lack of care by a previous owner.

The woodwork does not suffer too much, although the veneer can sometimes start to split, particularly around the instruments. This is not normally due to bad ownership but merely to the passage of time. You can buy complete wood sets for these cars either direct from Jaguar or from other sources, but this is again another area of cost to consider when buying.

The hood on Convertible models should be checked. With constant use the external covering will scar whilst the interior headlining will stain and mark easily. Regular cleaning should rectify this sort of thing. On the mechanical side mention is made in another chapter about the gelling of the hydraulic fluid used in the earlier models, which will either slow down or prevent the function of the hood mechanism. If this is the case when you check out a car, you should certainly demand that it is rectified before you buy.

Electrics

The electrics are far more long-lived than on previous Jaguars, but when looking to buy a car check that everything works, and correctly – though it may not necessarily be the item that doesn't work properly that is at fault: with modern multiplexing the source of a problem could lie anywhere within the car's electrical system and might require specialist advice to put right.

Normal problem areas relate to indicators double-flashing, instrument bulb failures, seat mechanism failures, electric window lift settings, and the multi-function steering column stalks becoming unable to adjust the on-board computer readouts. Only the last is a bit expensive as it usually entails replacing the speedometer instrument pack.

The headlamps are renowned for collecting and holding condensation. A dealer 'fix' has been to drill a very small hole in the rear side of the lamp unit and plug it with a vented grommet.

Mechanicals

The first major concern affects the pre-2000 model year cars carrying specific VIN numbers (see Chapter Nine for full information). The earlier engines used a Nikasil cylinder bore lining which has been known to degrade, eventually leading to total loss of compression and the need for a new engine. If buying a car equipped thus, you should carry out certain checks:

1. Is it still the original engine as identified on the registration document (which can be checked with a Jaguar dealership)?
2. If so, has the car recently had a blow-by test to check the engine compression?
3. If it is a replacement engine, does it have the correct identification tag (see next chapter and the picture on the right), or can you see that the engine block is painted grey?

If the answer to question 1 is yes, and even if it has had a blow-by test, it is reasonable to ask that such a test be carried out again, with written documentation to prove the figures, even if you agree to pay the small cost involved *if* the test results are satisfactory. Again, see the next chapter for further information on what the blow-by test should indicate.

If it is claimed that the engine is a Jaguar direct replacement, it may have lost its tag or the colour of the block may be difficult to determine – in which case you should enquire about proof in the form of an invoice, or details about the Jaguar dealership that carried out the change. Again, if this is not forthcoming then a blow-by test should be carried out.

As a general rule the car should start easily first time, hot or cold, and run evenly and supply good performance without hesitation. If any of these characteristics don't apply to a car you are testing, then further investigation should be carried out before purchasing.

Similarly, listen for rattles from the engine, particularly on start-up, which could be attributable to a failing timing chain tensioner, another common

The correct replacement engine tag fitted by Jaguar if an engine has been changed. The tags sometimes go missing, and even the colour of the engine block won't always help, so paperwork is vital if buying a car with a supposed engine change. (Nigel Thorley)

problem with these engines and covered in the next chapter. Also, check that the cooling system is in good condition and that there are no acrid smells of coolant or signs of leaking (the water pumps are prone to disintegrating). Rattles from underneath at the rear on earlier cars nearly always relate to handbrake cables, easy to rectify but annoying to hear.

A good solid service history should relieve a lot of concerns, and it is worth checking with previous owners or the appropriate Jaguar dealership about a car's past history before you part with your money. Concerning mileage, it is still generally considered that a low-mileage car is best for the obvious reason that it has had less wear and tear, but with today's highly sophisticated vehicles this is not necessarily the case. A high-mileage car, in constant use, can provide superb transport for many miles without trouble. The longer an XK remains unused, the more likely there are to be minor, and in some cases major, problems through flat batteries (which on being recharged bring up more major issues), tyres going 'square' through the constant weight standing on one area, corroded brake discs through lack of use, etc, etc. A higher mileage car, with a good service history, can often be a much better buy and, of course, will cost less than a very low-mileage example. Worth thinking about!

Many early cars suffered from a worn bush in the throttle housing caused by the cable being dislodged and causing unnecessary wear. A factory 'fix' was to fit a cable tie, and by now this should have been carried out on all cars.

Then there is the issue of the timing chain tensioners, which can often be heard on earlier cars as a slight rattle on start-up (not always the case, though). It is a good idea to establish if the top tensioner has been changed, which should be substantiated by an appropriate invoice for the work.

Look for irregular tyre wear too, particularly at the front which could be indicative of worn ball joints, a very common fault on these cars which can result in other major repair work. It is also usual for the steering to be knocked out of track more easily than with other cars. This can be determined by the feel of the steering (it will pull to one side) and, of course, by uneven tyre wear.

Bushes and shock absorbers will cause the most common problems with regular use – all easily dealt with, although you should bear in mind that if the car is equipped with CATS suspension then special and expensive shock absorbers are the order of the day.

In conclusion

There are always plenty of cars for sale. Have a clear idea of what you are looking for, let your budget dictate, learn as much about the car(s) as you can, take expert advice, and take your time.

Chapter **Nine**

Owning, running and caring for your XK8

An overview

Although the technology in most earlier Jaguar models can be attributed to conventional engineering, electrical practice and construction, things started to change dramatically for the company after the Ford takeover. The X-300 saloons (1994 to 1997) saw the introduction of new technology and improved build quality, and when the AJ-V8-engined cars came along they had a major impact and caused somewhat of a technological revolution.

The V8-engined cars are therefore very different to previous models in virtually all areas. For example, there is very little component interchangeability between the XK8 and any previous Jaguar models except for the floorpan (carried over from the XJS). Front suspension, steering, etc. are all very different, although the rear axle and handbrake mechanism owe their origins to the XJ40 saloon introduced in 1986. The XK8 is therefore a product of today's world, much better in many respects but nevertheless built to price, and concentrating on lightness and ease of parts replacement.

The concept of construction has also changed dramatically since the early 1990s. Safety issues relating to impacts and emissions controls, etc. have all played their part in forcing Jaguar, like other car manufacturers, down a route which complicates matters for enthusiasts wishing to work on these cars. Certain equipment areas are now compartmentalised for safety – for example, the vacuum brake servo booster, the reservoir plus appropriate ECU, the relays, etc. are all housed within plastic cases with covers. These make the engine bay look cleaner but inevitably mean more work at repair time.

One of the first things that XK enthusiasts must realise, therefore, is that these are not the easiest vehicles for a DIY mechanic to work on. Whilst servicing and some other maintenance work is quite possible, other, more involved work is not only very complex but awkward, requiring specialist tools which, by virtue of cost, don't make it viable for the average home-maintenance mechanic to buy them on the rare occasions they may be needed. The factory equivalent of workshop manuals don't exist for XK models, and although the Jaguar Daimler Heritage Trust now offer CDs of parts and service supplementary information, this material is rather scant and, at the time of writing, only covers the earlier models.

Alternatively there is the Jaguar Global Technical Reference website at www.jaguartechinfo.com, a subscription website which is quite comprehensive and includes technical information on the XK range.

SAFETY ISSUES

Before commencing any work on a car, certain measures should be taken to ensure maximum safety:

- Never work underneath a car supported only on jacks.
- If working underneath, ensure the car is located on solid level ground and supported on sufficiently strong axle stands situated in the correct positions under the vehicle.
- If only raising part of the car, ensure that the wheels still on the ground are secured by chocks.
- Only use equipment suitable for working on a specialist and heavy car like the XK.
- When carrying out any electrical work, disconnect the battery earth terminal in the boot.
- Wear effective clothing that is both safe for you and unlikely to cause damage to the vehicle.

Service schedules, instructions and other worthwhile information can be found there.

Engines

Modern technology and construction methods, however, have their advantages. The engines are very compact, making for ease of access. Even the fitment of a supercharger on XKR models does not hinder access

Examples of early (1996) and late (2005) XK8 engine bays, the latter, of course, of 4.2-litre capacity. (Nigel Thorley)

too much, and indeed, the R engines are essentially the same as the normally aspirated versions in so many ways that one should not be afraid of buying an XKR just because it 'appears' more complex. The engines are designed and assembled well, but some of the execution is probably not as good as with earlier, more basic units.

These well thought-out engines are built to facilitate economy and weight-saving, so in construction the lower section is actually a complete cross-cast web, milled to form the main bearing housing. This entire 'web' bolts to the underside of the cylinder block, like pre-war cars with a separate crankcase, blocks and heads. Items such as the valves and springs are lighter and a fraction of the size of traditional engines of similar capacity, so engines rev higher pushing less weight around which means more power.

Extensive use is also made of plastic components, which have strengths and weaknesses. Very light and easy to mould into weird and wonderful shapes, they are economic to produce and fit and are better insulators against noise. Even items like the inlet manifolds are plastic. On the downside, the longevity of plastic parts has sometimes been called into question, particularly as regards regular wear in items like timing chain tensioners, or where plastic covers and parts have to be frequently removed and replaced.

The interchangeability of V8 engines in later life is fraught with problems. If you need a replacement it is vital you get hold of the exact type of engine for the exact XK model. It isn't, for example, easily possible to fit an S-type 4.0-litre unit to an XK8, or even to fit an XK8 engine not built to accept an oil cooler into a car that has one. Even items like the sump changed according to model application.

Modern engines are also full of electronic equipment and sensors. The days of the simple distributor and HT leads has long gone. Instead, AJ-V8s have eight individual ignition coils, one above each spark plug; there is no distributor and all ignition mapping is done through ECU inputs. This is where the sensors come in, such as the Crankshaft Speed Sensor (assessing engine speed), the Camshaft Position Sensor (at the back – some have two), the Knock Sensors (one per cylinder bank), the Engine Coolant Sensor, the Air Temperature Sensor, and the various other emissions control components, dependent on which world market the car was originally built for.

Items like the throttle body assembly are also to some extent over-engineered and very complex compared to previous models and require care when handling or attempting to work on them. Then there are the exhaust systems, gases passing through catalysts in the downpipe assemblies with one or more oxygen sensors – and so it goes on.

Regarding the supercharged engines, again the whole design and installation has been very well thought out and engineered, so these shouldn't frighten anyone. Jaguar chose the gear type of supercharger, essentially a gear pump, rotating one set via the engine which in turn drives another set, all of which are superbly machined. The system works by forcing air into the engine, compressing it and giving it greater density and therefore greater mass. Put very simply, a greater mass of air forced into the engine allows for more fuel to be injected and therefore a bigger 'bang' is created, so the car goes faster. The air becomes exceptionally hot so intercoolers (one per inlet manifold) are there to cool it – so hot, in fact, that it relies on the engine coolant itself to keep the air 'cool'. Finally there is one electric water pump pumping coolant around the intercooler circuit. It sounds complicated but it is, in fact, a very simple principle that has been used many times before in motoring history and is a very reliable way of extracting more power from the engine.

It must be pointed out that the compression ratio for the supercharged engines is much lower than a normally aspirated unit, which again means that you can't replace an R engine with an 8 unit, or vice versa.

There are also a couple of strategically vital issues concerning the longevity of the earlier V8 engines fitted to both XK8 and XKR cars, so important that they are featured separately and in detail here.

Nikasil engine linings

As the new AJ-V8 engines were built for lightness, a new Nikasil (nickel silicon carbide) coating was used instead of conventional cylinder bore sleeves in order to save weight. BMW had experienced some problems with this type of lining earlier, but Jaguar felt that with their new-technology engines with fast warm-up times similar problems would not apply. Also, they had not experienced problems during the extensive testing of V8 engines in the XK8 prior to launch.

However, it later became evident that the Nikasil lining could degrade, which was primarily put down to the use of high levels of sulphur in the fuel. In these circumstances sulphur is converted into a corrosive substance during the combustion process, which then

causes erosion to the bore lining. Jaguar then identified that the problem was only associated with the UK market (although cases have since been recorded elsewhere), and even within the UK there were 'hot-spots' which led to worse problems than elsewhere. But of course, the movement of cars through different owners and countries cancels the geographical aspect out somewhat.

Since January 2000 the sulphur content in fuels has been eliminated, but the problem nevertheless still crops up in earlier engines after a time. It can also be aggravated by the type of use the engine is subjected to. For example, a very high mileage example, driven for consistently long periods, is a less likely candidate for problems than a car that merely covers a minimal mileage (mainly on a cold engine).

The symptoms relating to this problem show in poor cold-starting and/or a general lack of performance, both of which can be attributed to low compression, a sure sign that the bores are worn. The ultimate test is to have a blow-by (airflow) test done by a specialist, who can determine and then compare the degree of engine breathing with the factory standard. Connecting an airflow meter to a warm engine determines the flow in litres per minute, the upper limit being 40 litres per minute; at this level or above it is considered best to change the engine, although in practical terms any figure above about 30 litres per minute should give cause for concern. In the region of 9 to 19 litres per minute is about normal for a good condition AJ-V8.

A very quick point of reference which can also highlight the incidence of premature bore wear is to remove the air filter assembly, and if this is found to contain oil then this can be attributed to the same problem.

Many early cars have already had replacement service-reconditioned engines fitted by Jaguar, and all post-2000 engines have conventional cast iron cylinder liners so this problem can never arise again. If your car doesn't have substantiated documentation to prove the fitment of a new engine, there is usually a special tag fitted to the nearside of the engine block to identify it and, of course, if the engine is a replacement then this number should be different to that shown on the original log sheet. Lastly, all reconditioned engines from Jaguar were apparently spray-painted a grey colour, though this may be difficult to determine on an engine in situ.

There are only a few viable rebuilt AJ-V8 engines available at the time of writing, outside of the Jaguar network, so the main source of supply is still Jaguar themselves, in the form of a replacement service exchange unit via a Jaguar dealership. Or you could purchase a used engine from one of the several Jaguar specialist breakers now taking in accident-damaged cars. But remember, the correct type of engine should be fitted to each specific XK model, or you may get involved in many problems that will take a considerable amount of time, and perhaps money, to rectify.

As the cars concerned are now getting older, there are fewer opportunities to gain redress from Jaguar Cars over the cost, or part cost, of engine replacement. This depends on previous ownership, mileage, and service history, and the only way to find out is to contact the Jaguar dealership from whom the car came or by which it has been maintained.

Typical example of a damaged secondary tensioner, with the covering breaking away from the metal shoe. (Nigel Thorley)

Timing chain tensioners

The engines suffer from breakage of the upper timing chain tensioners. Any cars that have received replacement engines supplied by Jaguar should already have been modified to a later style of tensioner, but probably of the plastic type. It could also be that the tensioners themselves have already been changed by a previous owner, but the only way to tell (without documented service history to support this) is to remove the cam covers and physically check.

The problem takes the form of either the main casing splitting and/or the plastic material over which the chain runs parting from the metal shoe itself. To make matters worse, as the plastic parts from the metal the shoe will break up. This will immediately cause the piston to extend further from the cylinder, so creating more side loading onto the housing body and increasing the propensity and speed at which it will crack. If the plastic comes away from the shoe the chain will run in the metal backing, and if allowed to continue the tensioners can break up completely, with disastrous results – the chain becomes jammed and breaks, at worst rendering the engine uneconomical to repair.

To add further complications there are also lower timing chain tensioners and plastic dampers which are far more inaccessible. These, however, tend to be more reliable, particularly as the chain does not ride directly over the lower tensioner. However, failure of these lower tensioners will create a pronounced rattling noise from the engine and when this occurs these

Chain and tensioner layout in the XK engine. (Nigel Thorley)

tensioners must be replaced, as breakage of the chain is possible. This is a much more involved job with obvious financial implications.

The only way to check the condition of these is by removing the camshaft covers, when the upper tensioners become easily visible. The lower ones require the use of a slimline torch to illuminate them from above. Generally speaking, if the primary chains (tensioned by the lower tensioners) are taut on both the tight and slack sides, the lower tensioners can be considered to be good, assuming there are no visible signs of mechanical damage.

It is possible to change the upper timing chain tensioners without removing any of the chains at all, which means that the job is a relatively inexpensive affair, consuming typically two to three hours of labour plus the cost of two new tensioners, plus a set of cam cover gaskets and seals. However, if the lower tensioners are also to be changed it becomes more than a full day's work, and including parts the cost will be considerably more.

Even though the secondary chains may be running on the metal of the upper timing chain tensioners, if after careful examination the chains appear to be alright, it is acceptable to merely change the tensioners. However, if the chains have become damaged – exhibited by a wearing of the surface of the chain where it meets the metal of the tensioner – it is possible (with the correct tools) to split and remove the damaged chain and replace it with a split-link unit. This negates the need to remove the primary chain and the obvious costs associated with such work.

If engine rattle is noticed on start-up, or there is resonance throughout certain speed bands, it is prudent to consider having the lower tensioners

Alternatively the tensioner main casing may split like this. (Nigel Thorley)

The various types of timing chain tensioner used on the V8 engines. The two at the top – both of which are damaged in some way – are examples of the original type fitted by Jaguar. The third is the first generation replacement, which was stronger and incorporated a useful clip-pull to release the spring when fitted. At the bottom is the very latest type, made of metal, which is likely to prove a better option all round for longevity. (Nigel Thorley)

checked. It isn't that difficult to do this work at home although some special tools are required (camshaft position setting tool, sprocket retaining tool, suitable short Allen key socket with an appropriately slimline torque wrench (reading up to 125Nm), plus a quality socket set), and when fitting the replacement tensioners it is important to realise that they are different for each side of the engine – if you fit the wrong tensioner to the wrong side, the engine will be damaged.

The work involves the removal of the electrical coils, air filter box, coolant expansion tank, and camshaft covers from both banks. With the top tensioners and timing chains in view, the engine has to be turned over by hand to a position allowing a special locking tool to be inserted over the camshafts. The exhaust camshaft sprocket is then removed, and after unbolting the tensioners they just lift free.

Tensioners have been upgraded over the years, the latest type, introduced in February 2005, being an aluminium-bodied version of the secondary (upper) tensioner. It is advised by many specialists that all engines equipped with plastic tensioners should really have them replaced with the new aluminium version as a matter of preventive maintenance.

With the cam cover off, using a long screwdriver, you can check the tension of the lower timing chain. If slack, this will need to be addressed.

In the overall scheme of things, looking after the tensioners is a moderately inexpensive job – particularly when compared to the cost of major engine repairs should a breakage occur.

The fuel system

A common occurrence with these engines relates to flooding. This is normally down to starting a car cold and moving it a very small distance before turning the engine off again. It is a problem with many modern cars and engines, and results from excess fuel in the bores flooding the engine. In many cases this can be overcome by flooring the accelerator, which informs the EMS to disable the fuel injectors momentarily so that when you crank the engine over (with the pedal depressed) the cylinders are vented and eventually the car will fire naturally. Alternatively, go to the fuse box in the boot and remove fuse No. 7, which disables the fuel pump. You can then crank the engine over at half-throttle, building up oil pressure to the point where the

Thermostat and seal for the V8 engine. Note the bleed hole giggle pin, which *must* be set to the 12 o'clock position when fitting.
(Nigel Thorley)

engine will momentarily fire for a few seconds, using up the fuel it has. Then, on reconnecting the fuse the engine will re-crank with the aid of a light throttle.

To avoid the problem, leave the car running for about five minutes to warm up before turning it off.

Cooling system

One of the Achilles heels of the V8 engine is the cooling system. It is actually a very efficient system, but there are some important issues with it and its construction. It could be said that modern lightweight materials let it down.

On the expansion tank there is a small Low Coolant Temperature Sensor at the bottom, so if the 'low coolant' light appears on the dashboard it is vital the level is checked immediately, because this warning doesn't come up quickly enough. The electrically controlled design of the temperature gauge provides for a midway point for 'driver comfort', so again is far from accurate. Also, by virtue of the temperature sensor's placement, some parts of the engine can get very hot whilst other areas (like the thermostat housing) can remain quite cool.

The expansion tanks bolt onto the inner wing and there are small bleed pipes that push-fit. It is not uncommon for these pipes to get caught, pulling them free, particularly as they become brittle on older engines. If detached, then again temperature readings will be affected.

Given all of this, there are two reasons for the engine to overheat: either the water pump or the thermostat will have failed. Signs to look out for (because of the inaccuracy of the warning systems) are the cooling fans staying on for long periods regardless of temperature, and/or one of the top hoses blowing off – particularly on normally aspirated cars – causing a sudden severe loss of coolant.

The thermostat housing has water outlets made of plastic which can cause problems with hoses blowing off. The hose clips used on these cars are actually spring clips, which require a special tool to undo them. Used for ease of manufacture and because they are quicker to undo and fit, on plastic housings they tend to lose tension, causing the hoses to blow off. The housings on supercharged engines are aluminium and therefore don't necessarily present the same problems.

The thermostat is of the conventional style thermos type with its own seal supplied. The thermostat has a bleed hole (giggle pin) to allow air to purge, so it is essential that this pin is set to the 12 o'clock position when fitting into the housing.

The water pumps have plastic impellers which disintegrate over time. A quick way to check is not to take the water pump off but simply, with a cold engine, take the filler cap off from the expansion tank, then run the engine at approximately 1,200rpm. If the pump is working correctly, water will be circulating quite briskly, causing a swirl of fluid from the bleed pipes back into the tank. If the pump isn't working, there will be little circulation and therefore hardly any swirl.

The water pump sits right at the front of engine below the pipes and housing. The seal beneath the bleed housing can also leak. The pump is fairly easy to change. The pulley is held in place by three 8mm bolts and it is best to undo these before de-tensioning the drive belt, as the one holds the other in place. When removing the belt it is best to inspect it for wear. The belt on supercharged engines doesn't actually need to be de-tensioned, but if it needs to be changed it is easier to remove the fan cowl as well.

With the belt removed, use a screwdriver or bar to ease off the water pump pulley. This will give access to five 8mm headed bolts that hold the pump in place. Undoing them allows the pump to be pulled out, being simply an O-ring fit into the aperture in the cylinder block. Once removed, the remains of the impeller blades will be seen and replacement is necessary. Replacements still have plastic (but improved) impellers and come with a modified gasket and no O-ring. A new thermostat should always be fitted if changing the water pump.

Severe overheating problems with these engines can lead to major bills, and the resultant damage can be amazing. Every care should be taken to prevent overheating. For example, the heater return and feed hoses pass underneath the manifold. They cost little to purchase but can take between one and three hours to replace dependent on the model. An unexplained coolant loss can often be attributed to the failure of one of these. It is not unknown for an engine to become so hot that it will melt a breather pipe.

Whilst not a common occurrence, these engines are in later life beginning to blow head gaskets. Any signs of heavy steam from the exhausts or a slight misfire on start-up (usually when cold) must be investigated further.

It is worth noting that from about the 2001 model year different compounds of antifreeze were used.

The all-important water pump for the V8 engine, clearly showing the plastic impellers which are the cause of many overheating problems. (Nigel Thorley)

Mixing this later type with earlier antifreeze can cause the coolant to gel, with inevitable consequences.

Gearboxes

The gearbox used up to 2003 in normally aspirated cars is a ZF five-speed unit, whereas the supercharged models use a Mercedes 'box as fitted to many larger-engined Mercedes cars. Both are very smooth in operation and don't usually give any problems up to 60,000 miles. However, beyond this point they can cause problems, ultimately resulting in expensive replacement.

The ZF 'boxes have a forward clutch pack with a retaining clip that wears through the pressed steel housing and eventually falls away. The initial symptom of this is a slippage between gears. Later, after a normal journey, upon restarting and selecting drive, the box will not engage. Applying some throttle, the gear will engage and 'bite' harshly. Often reverse gear is still available. Not everything may be lost, however, as the same symptoms could be brought about by a blocked oil filter preventing oil passing through the gearbox.

The Mercedes gearbox on the R models has a problem with its output shaft assemblies and planetary sets breaking up. Early 'boxes had an alloy housing with little support, and over time the gear set started to move, the bearing eventually boring its way through the housing and dropping away, allowing the gears to lock up and break through the casing. This could also lock up the differential. So much debris is created during the wear process that the gearbox filter will clog up. This causes the gearbox to produce a whirring noise and/or slippage in some of the gears, which can be taken as an early warning of impending doom.

The gearboxes are supposedly a non-serviceable item, which means 'sealed for life'. However, you can buy – either from Jaguar or other suppliers – both gearbox sump gaskets and oil filters. Entirely new gearboxes from Jaguar can cost several thousand pounds, but many gearbox specialists now offer remanufactured units.

The normally aspirated 'box does not have a conventional dipstick or filler plug. Instead there is a small plug on the side through which oil is injected via a syringe pump (done when the engine is cold) until it overflows. This has to be done from underneath with the car on level ground, so it can be awkward for anyone to carry out at home without a pit or ramp. Also, the oil needed is quite special (Esso LT7 1141) and expensive, although it is possible to buy exactly the same oil for less money from specialists. It is vital, however, that only this oil is used to avoid unnecessary damage to the 'box.

Whilst the supercharged gearbox does have a dipstick tube, there is no dipstick. It is supplied as a special tool to Jaguar dealerships (and any independent specialists who purchased one), and it is by the use of this that the gearbox level is ascertained.

It is strongly advised that at around 50,000 miles the oil is drained, the sump pan removed, and the filter and oil replaced along with a new sump pan gasket. This will decidedly help to prolong the life of these gearboxes, at little expense.

Bearing in mind the high cost of the major 60,000-mile service, it is a good idea to opt for the gearbox work at 50,000 miles, which will save some expenditure later. By regular servicing, however, the life expectancy of both gearboxes can be much improved.

The normally aspirated ZF transmission has a range sensor switch, which sends signals to the engine control modules indicating what gear is selected and relates this to the ECU. These switches can be affected by water ingress creating erroneous signals that may show up on the dashboard message centre, such as 'overheating', 'gearbox failure', 'restricted performance', etc. This is not necessarily the terminal problem the message would indicate. Often £200 spent on a new switch can cure the symptom, but initially a

Jaguar dealer or good independent's diagnostic equipment will identify the source of the problem. The Mercedes gearboxes do not have a rotary switch on the gearbox. Instead a linear switch within the gear select quadrant is fitted, inside the car.

Another problem affecting the ZF gearboxes is the need to remove oil cooler pipes with threaded unions, which are made from aluminium and can easily seize, making them difficult to remove. They can shear, or it may be necessary to cut the pipe from underneath. It can take up to three hours to change these and there is the possibility of damage to the gearbox casing. Again, the Mercedes 'boxes use conventional banjo joints, so preventing the above problems.

There are no known problems at present with the very late six-speed ZF boxes.

Front suspension

The XK uses a very special aluminium subframe arrangement, different to any previous Jaguar. One of the problems here is that the steel bolts used to fit it to the car can seize in position. The XK also uses a different style of subframe mounting, with a 'V' mount at the rear and round one at the front. The former is known to split, but a set of long Torx-headed sockets is required to undo the bolts – access is difficult.

The lower wishbone arm is an integral unit with the ball joint. A new arm from Jaguar is very expensive, but they can be reconditioned. However, because of the angle at which the ball joint is pressed into the arm specialist equipment is needed to replace it. As a matter of course it is suggested that if changing the ball joints and bushes, then the front bushes should be changed at the same time.

The bushes are unique and need care in replacement. Note that there are two different part numbers, those ending with the suffix CA fit on the front lower wishbone, while those ending with BB are for the rear lower wishbone. Beware: they look exactly the same but are subtly different. The top wishbone bushes are of the slip-flex type, similar to but not interchangeable with those used on many earlier cars, such as the XJ Series.

The shock absorber and spring arrangement is also an integrated part, but uniquely the diameter of the spring is different top to bottom. There is a bush at the bottom of the shock absorber which is easily changeable when worn.

Wheel bearings at the front are very difficult to change because of the need for special tools, but their

The ABS rotor nut securing the hub and the special tool needed to undo it, the only means to remove it without damage. (Nigel Thorley)

This is no joke – this can be the amount of leverage required to remove the rotor nut to replace a front wheel bearing of an XK8! (Nigel Thorley)

maintenance is a very important issue. When they start to deteriorate and cause excess noise they should be changed immediately. The longer the worn bearing is left the harder it will be to change, and it could ultimately lead to other more expensive repairs. You can identify a worn wheel bearing by a constant drone at the front of the car accompanied by the feel, even through the steering wheel. The noise gets worse as you turn the steering as well.

Although the wheel bearings are easy to assemble from the manufacturer's point of view, being a one-piece housing with integrated bearing, when it comes to later replacement they are difficult. Removing the wheel housing appears to be a simple matter of removing the upright, undoing the nut, removing the calliper and disc to get to the hub, and taking out the bearing. However, the bottom ball joint taper fit is very tight – extremely so – and in the worst cases has to be cut off. The ABS rotor nut has to be removed, which secures the hub through the bearing and has a series of castellations on it for the wheel speed sensor to pick up. The sensor has to be removed, which is very expensive to replace. The rotor nut also requires a special socket to undo it. This is a non-wear item, so should clean up well.

The leverage required to undo the very tightly fitted bolt is enormous. On reassembly it is tightened to

220Nm – imagine what a few years of use, water ingress, etc. will do for the loosening torque required.

After all this the bearing has to be pressed out of its carrier – again in principle not difficult, but some force is required, and a special cradle is helpful to secure it in position. Two special circlips hold the bearing in situ, which should always be replaced and fitted to the same orientation, that is, pointing down.

Another area to check is the power steering cooler, which fails regularly. It is not difficult to change, but on the feed side there is a high pressure union, like a bayonet fixing which requires another special tool to separate.

Rear suspension

Though based on a design going back to the XJ40 saloons of the late 1980s, the differentials are of a different construction and are far longer-lived and mostly trouble free. But unlike earlier models there are complications due to the revised construction and installation of the new axle. For example, if you need to change the rear shock absorbers you have to unbolt and lower the rear suspension completely a few inches, and require a special (slim) spring compressor in order to release the shock absorber from its integrated spring. To do this necessitates undoing the rear tie bar, removing the A-frame safety plate, and unbolting the nuts holding the top plate of the shock absorber spring pan.

Then, with the spring compressed, the fulcrum pin must be removed, which can also be problematic as they seize in situ. In worst-case scenarios the bolts have to be cut off. Being difficult to access as well means you need a small angle grinder to do this work.

There is another issue relating to those cars fitted with the CATS active suspension system. Each shock absorber has an electrical connection which goes to the main wiring loom. Over time the shock absorbers actually 'rotate' in service, which can cause these electrical connections to wind and eventually pull off, in some cases necessitating their replacement, which again means dropping the rear suspension as a complete item.

Again, safety precautions _must_ be adhered to. Although a very slim coil spring compressor is needed for the rear of the XK, it is vital that it is of a substantial design fit for its purpose. (Nigel Thorley)

As mentioned in the text, removing the fulcrum pin at the rear is hampered by lack of space, particularly with a spring compressor in the way. Here a small angle grinder has to be used to cut it free. (Nigel Thorley)

When fitting new shock absorbers, the liberal use of copper grease will prevent squeaks when back in service. The lower section of the spring terminates in a pigtail, which must seat correctly with the end of the wishbone forging. If not done correctly, the ride height is affected and the spring can dislodge when on the road.

This leads us to the issue of the A-frame bushes, which will deteriorate over time. It is vital when replacing these to 'lock' them in with a suitable adhesive or they _will_ work loose and deform, allowing the A-frame to rest metal to metal in its mountings.

Brakes

Like most modern cars, all XK8s feature all-round disc brakes, which these days are more prone to wear due to our driving habits, greater reliance on brakes, and even the harder materials used in the production brake pads. As such the discs rarely last for more than 30,000 miles and, dependent on model, they can be expensive to replace.

Symptoms of the discs being in poor condition are a vibration through the steering wheel under braking, a juddering or pulsating through the brake pedal, or the brakes just being less effective, with greater pedal travel. An inspection of the discs with the road wheels off the car may also reveal severely corroded areas around the edge of the discs (which might be eating into the face), bad pitting on the face, and severe uneven-wear ridges,

It is vital that the rear spring seats correctly with the wishbone forging. (Nigel Thorley)

all of which dictate that the discs need changing. They should always be changed in pairs.

They are not difficult or time-consuming to change by removing the calliper body. With the old disc removed, it is important to clean up the hub so that the new disc will mate true with it when reassembled. The callipers should also be thoroughly cleaned, and always fit new pads when the discs are changed. The callipers' securing bolts should be thread-locked to ensure they don't come loose.

The handbrake cable mechanism is very much based on the XJS and it is quite common to find them incorrectly adjusted, in the worst case leading to the cable snapping. Cheap and relatively easy to replace, this also brings up a common fault with XK8s – that the cables rattle on the road.

Only three bolts (two with important spacers you must not lose) secure the handbrake mechanism to the interior floor. To remove the old cable you also have to lift the one-piece carpeting which, for ease, necessitates undoing the seat slide on the driver's side. Good access is also required underneath the car, necessitating either a ramp, pit or heavy duty axle stands on which to support the rear. The new cable should be fitted at the handbrake lever end first to optimise the free play inside the car, not forgetting to secure it with the retaining clip provided.

On the underside of the floorpan a large rubber grommet provides access to the location hole through which the handbrake passes into the car. Afterwards this grommet must be replaced properly to prevent ingress of water into the car.

Regular servicing

Service intervals are 10,000 miles for all engines, although the work required will vary according to which 10,000 service it is and whether it is a normally aspirated or supercharged engine. A full schedule of servicing work is shown in Appendix D.

Most aspects of general servicing can be addressed by the average, competent DIY home mechanic, and you can buy service kits from a Jaguar dealer which provide all the items you require, including a disposable seat cover! The cost of many service components is certainly not expensive, although when it comes to items like the spark plugs, these don't come cheap. It is more cost effective to buy a kit rather than the individual items, though you will, of course, have to buy all the fluids required as well.

A standard 10,000-mile service involves little more than oil, filter and wiper blade changes and a visual check of other things. At 30,000 miles it gets a little more costly with supercharged and early normally aspirated engines, as they will need the spark plugs changing later. This applies to later normally aspirated engines at 60,000 miles. At this point other items, such as the fuel filter, need changing too, so it becomes more expensive overall.

You can tackle the order of service work in many ways so this is merely a guide. Firstly, the normal principle of jacking up the front end of the car to gain access to and drain the engine sump doesn't apply here. The 13mm sump plug is positioned right at the front of the engine facing down. Draining with the car jacked up at the front will mean that not all the oil will be removed. So you jack up the *back* of the car instead. Ensure that the front wheels are chocked before jacking. The rear of the car must be supported on axle stands before any work is carried out underneath.

The oil filter on the AJ-V8 engine is somewhat obscured by an alternator cooling duct, force-feeding air to keep it cool. If the car has been well maintained this duct will still be there and will need removing by undoing the bolt, to gain easy access to the filter.

While the oil is left to thoroughly drain, your attention can be switched to the rear of the car, still supported on axle stands. The A-frame supporting the rear suspension and axle is of a similar design to that used on Jaguar saloons. Check its bushes to ensure they have not degraded or collapsed. Although much longer-lived than those used on other models, they will needs to be checked for distortion or cracking, as it will induce vibration or, at worst, come loose, damaging the companion flange or even the propshaft itself. If this has been changed or needs to be changed, it is vital it is fitted the correct way round, identified by an arrow cast into the rubber. This arrow dictates the direction in which the bolts should pass (back to front), and therefore the direction of fit.

The rear suspension bump stops should always be checked to ensure that they are firmly secured. The metal backing never comes away but the rubber will de-bond. Pull any de-bonding off if loose, or it could fly

All that is required for a standard 10,000-mile service of the Jaguar V8 engine, supplied as a 'kit' from a Jaguar dealership. (Nigel Thorley)

still deteriorate over time and should be inspected at every service.

Then there is the rotoflex coupling, a rayon-reinforced rubber mounting at the gearbox end of the propshaft that reduces harmonics inside the car. This

The alternator cooling duct being removed to reveal the oil filter (white) above. The front of the sump-mounted oil drain plug is arrowed. (Nigel Thorley)

DISCONNECTING THE BATTERY

The battery should be disconnected before carrying out any electrical work. The battery is sited under the boot floor, access being gained by removal of the right-hand panel. The battery can be disconnected via the 10mm bolt negative earth connection. Ensure you fold the terminal firmly underneath or away from the battery so that it won't spring back at some point later on and form a connection and spark that could prove disastrous.

You also need to be aware that it is not unknown for the car doors to self-lock once the battery is reconnected, so always remove the ignition keys from the car when working on it. The boot lid also has an electronic release, from the dashboard on all models and from the boot lid plinth on later cars. So if the car does self-lock when the battery is reconnected, and then you close the boot lid, how are you going to get in if you did leave the keys in the ignition? There is a conventional keyhole within the 'XK' badge on the boot lid, but few people ever use it so the lock often corrodes inside or gets filled with debris from the road and seizes up.

As well as removing the keys from the ignition, another way to avoid locking yourself out is to 'throw' the boot latch with the aid of a screwdriver or similar so that the boot lid can't close at all until you release the lock when you have finished. Otherwise you could end up having to remove the number plate and drill the boot lid to gain access to the release mechanism!

A final point on batteries: if a battery goes flat on an XK, don't jumpstart the car from another battery on a vehicle with its engine running. This could lead to a spike in the electrical circuits that could have disastrous and expensive results somewhere. Always remove the offending battery, charge it off the car and then refit it, or just disconnect both terminal leads so it is isolated from the car while charging.

The A-frame bushes at the rear can easily be visually checked for condition. (Nigel Thorley)

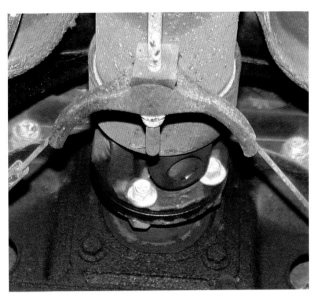

The rotoflex coupling on the propshaft should always be checked when servicing these cars. (Nigel Thorley)

out and cause problems for other road-users. There are different types of bump stop for different models, so ensure you get the right one for your car.

A visual check can be carried out to ensure that the springs have not become dislodged from their seats, and by exerting pressure on the rear wings (when the car is back on the ground) you can determine the condition of the shock absorbers.

On to the rear brakes. The handbrake cross brace area is essentially the same as that used on previous saloons. The fulcrum pin is prone to seizing, but the regular and liberal use of a release agent should help. Using an impact gun to revolve it, you can check it is completely free. If it isn't or hasn't been free the handbrake shoes will remain against the drum part of the disc/drum assembly, causing overheating and, perhaps, de-bonding of the shoe material, which can drop into the drum. Shoes are expensive to replace.

Conventional vented discs are fitted to all XKs (unless they have had R-Performance Brembos fitted) using conventional Teves sliding callipers. Life expectancy of discs varies dramatically with driver and type of driving, but they will inevitably have been changed on even very late examples by now (see earlier comments on visual checks of discs and callipers). The subject of changed discs at the rear brings up another issue regarding effective maintenance.

There is a small access port in the drum to allow for handbrake adjustment. Time and again discs have been changed and the access hole not lined up with

the adjuster, because the discs will fit in any position over the studs. As you have to slacken off the handbrake shoes to remove a disc, you need to retighten them again when the new disc is fitted, but you can't if the holes don't line up – an excellent example of possible poor maintenance.

Adjusting the handbrake from underneath the car provides an improvement over XJSs via a self-locking nut at the end of a threaded rod passing through the compensator assembly. It is important not to over-adjust as the shoes will remain on and will grab.

Another visual check at the rear should involve the exhaust system. Whilst generally long-lasting, the rear silencers are prone to corrosion on all models.

Checking the condition of the rear bump stops. (Nigel Thorley)

With the wheel removed, the rear brakes and suspension assembly can be seen. A visual check of the disc should determine its condition. The suspension bump stop and the A-frame bushes can also be easily seen and checked at this point. (Nigel Thorley)

The access port in the drum for handbrake adjustment. (Nigel Thorley)

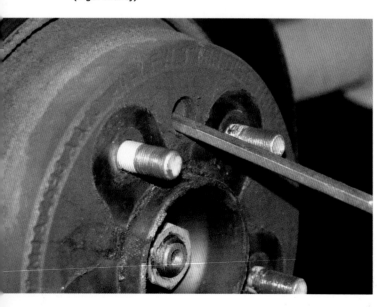

For safety, the fuel filter is these days tucked away under the floor towards the rear on the left hand side. Inaccessible due to exhaust heat shields, it can be awkward to remove.

You can depressurise the system by running the car and pulling fuse No. 7 from the boot-mounted fuse box. This de-energizes the pump and the pressure will fall off. When replacing the fuel filter, it only goes on one way, shown by the arrows on the casing.

The rubbers on the rear anti-roll bar can fail, causing a 'chatter' from the back of the car. The drop links don't fail in service but the nuts and locking compounds attaching them are prone to seizure over time, and the studs can break. If you need to replace a drop link, bear in mind that they're easy to break, so it is advisable to do such a job when you can get access to new parts.

There is no drain plug on the differential casing and even getting at the filler plug is difficult because of the anti-roll bar and strengthening bar across the axle. Ideally use a socket with a small extension bar, and the car must be level but far enough off the ground to do it. All the differentials take a new synthetic 65/90 grade oil or similar, but for top-up purposes a conventional 90 grade is alright to use.

Despite the modernity of the XK there are still four grease nipples to look after, two on each half-shaft, one on each universal joint. Often neglected (another sign of poor maintenance), access is easy and normal grease can be used. At service intervals they should be checked for play, although you should first carry out any greasing required. Also check the outer fulcrum and rear wheel bearings. It isn't possible to grease either the wheel bearings or the outer fulcrums. Life expectancy for these is quite long, usually in excess of 100,000 miles.

Checking for play should not only be done in the six o'clock and twelve o'clock positions, but also at three and nine o'clock as well. Changing the outer fulcrum is difficult as the races are awkward to get out if seriously corroded, in some cases necessitating cutting them out.

Still underneath the car, working methodically towards the front, you should also regularly check the fuel and brake lines, thoroughly wax-protecting them against corrosion. Unfortunately the modern materials used for these lines are not as long-lived as on many older vehicles, and although it is not within the normal Jaguar service schedule to carry out any waxing, it is a worthwhile task which improves longevity. The waxing

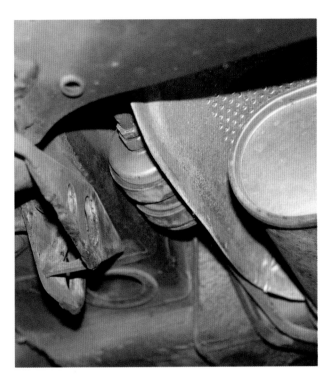

This is the fuel filter position underneath the XK8. (Nigel Thorley)

Regular checking of brake and fuel lines is important with so much salt on the roads during the winter, particularly in the UK. (Nigel Thorley)

Not only is it important to regularly check the condition and wear of tyres, but when replacing the alloy wheels it is important to grease the faces where they come into contact with the hubs, to prevent them 'sticking' metal to metal. (Nigel Thorley)

should also be done in and around the brackets securing the pipes, as the lines will still corrode in such places if not protected.

All XK8 models were designed around the use of Pirelli tyres of the appropriate size, although these may have been replaced at some time by previous owners. All tyres should be checked for uneven wear, which will provide valuable information on current or previous problems with steering, ball joints or suspension issues.

As all XKs were equipped with alloy wheels the inner face mating to the hub should always be greased before fitting. The alloy wheel nuts should always be tightened with a torque wrench to 75lb ft. If the wheels are fitted too tightly, damage to the wheel nuts, the wheels, or even the locking nut (one per wheel) can occur. Whilst on the subject of wheels, these should always be checked for damage.

Tyre pressures vary according to type of driving and the tyres. With Pirelli, about 32psi will normally provide a good comfortable ride. Space saver spares, where fitted, should always be maintained at a pressure of 60psi. When using a space saver a car cannot be driven at more than 50mph.

Returning to the front end, now that the oil has completely drained it is useful, in some circumstances, to consider removing the sump pan to clean out the internals. This is recommended if the oil is particularly

The correct way to check for play in the lower ball joints: with the car supported on axle stands, jack the lower wishbone until a crowbar can be used between the tyre and the ground to check for play in the ball joint. (Nigel Thorley)

dirty or there are indications of deposits built up inside the engine. Unlike some other Jaguar models, sump removal is not hindered by cross members or other items. You should remember to use a new gasket if doing this job, to ensure a good seal afterwards. When replacing the sump plug, before refilling the engine with oil, a new washer should always be fitted (supplied with the Jaguar service kit). The same applies to the oil filter.

When filling engines with oil use a funnel because the neck of the filler is low down and it is easy to spill oil onto one of the coil housings or a catalyst and exhaust manifold. The type of oil for a normally aspirated V8 is a semi-synthetic 10/40 grade, and for a supercharged engine Castrol Magnatec 5/30 is recommended.

Now the rear of the car can be lowered, and the front end raised to carry out other inspections, such as the

ball joints. A visual sign of their failure can be identified by extreme inner-edge tyre wear. An important point here is to jack up the car the correct way.

Jack up the front of the car so that the wheels are just touching the ground and support it on axle stands. Place a jack under the lower suspension wishbone, as close to the wheel as possible, and jack the suspension until a crowbar or large flat screwdriver can be inserted between the ground and the tyre. Gently lever the wheel upwards and watch for any play in the ball joint between the wheel hub carrier and the lower wishbone. Any play indicates that the ball joint is worn.

Front wheel bearings are a regular area of concern with these cars and most of the time don't last beyond 30,000 miles. As mentioned earlier, special procedures are required for this work.

As with the rear, check the brake callipers for smooth operation and the discs for damage or wear. If you need to remove any callipers, they are held in place by two Allen-headed screws at the back. Undoing these and removing the spring clip at the front allows the calliper to be withdrawn. Check the disc faces front and back for corrosion: they start to corrode on the inner edge outwards and outer edge inwards and are always worst on the inside face. These brake discs should not be skimmed and are expensive to replace.

Check the power-steering reservoir, which should always remain full. Leaks here are not common. Also check the windscreen washer reservoir, but do not spill any fluid when replenishing as it can enter wiring around this area.

These engines don't take (or use) a lot of coolant compared to older cars – about 8 litres maximum – which should always be maintained at a 50/50 mix of water to antifreeze. Replenishment is carried out via the expansion tank filler in the engine bay. Note that there are bleed plugs within the centre of the engine which must be undone to purge air from the system. Beware that around 2001 Jaguar introduced a long-life antifreeze solution, and if your car is so provided you should not mix it with other types of antifreeze, which can cause gelling of the coolant.

Radiators should be periodically drained and flushed out to remove debris, not just from the internal area but also from the core using a high-pressure water jet. It is just possible to reach the drain tap, on the right at the base of the radiator, from the top of the engine bay but access is very fiddly. Once undone, the coolant will release everywhere, causing some mess around the front valance, which will need cleaning off afterwards. It may be that the radiator will need removing from the car for closer inspection and to remove ingrained debris from the core. Whilst relatively simple on a normally aspirated car, it is an awkward job on supercharged versions.

Onto other engine components. To start with, pay particular attention to the condition of the main drive belt at the front. The Jaguar service schedule dictates that this should be changed at 60,000-mile intervals, but for safety always check it at 40,000 miles. If it has started to crack, it must be changed immediately. A strange noise from the front of the engine can often be attributed to this belt breaking up – as the pulleys rotate, the 'missing' part of the belt creates the noise.

The belt is of a serpentine design with an extensive run, driving many different components of the engine. It takes its maximum grip over the crankshaft pulley and the highest load over the alternator. There is an additional belt on the supercharged models around the crankshaft pulley to the supercharger. This makes it more difficult to change because it passes through a

This main drive belt is breaking up badly with part of the inside core now disappearing. (Nigel Thorley)

The main drive belt is easily removable by rotating this tensioner counter-clockwise via this 15mm bolt. (Nigel Thorley)

The inserts in the engine covers tend to come away and get lost. (Nigel Thorley)

plastic covers, all of which need to be removed to change the spark plugs. The covers are secured to the engine by six 7mm headed bolts. Four of these are easy to access, but two are fiddly and are sometimes missing on poorly serviced cars. You will need a good-quality ¼in drive socket set, also useful for other areas of maintenance on these cars. There are small inserts on the covers which tend to pull out with the bolts. Using a pair of mole grips, take them off the bolts and replace them in the covers to avoid losing them.

Removing the covers provides access to the four coils per bank. Disconnect the wires (quite idiot-proof as the wiring loom is a tailored fit). The coils are held in place by 7mm bolts. You will need to disconnect the electrical connectors first. The coils lift out, being directly above the spark plugs. Once removed for the first time or changed, interference on FM reception can often be encountered. Removing the coil, pulling off the rubber boots to clean the metal at the base of the coil and stretching the spring will make contact better and relieve the interference.

narrow gap around the tensioner, so it can prove easier to remove the tensioner first.

Removing the belt involves rotating a left-hand threaded 15mm bolt towards the centre of the engine. This is done using a suitably long combination spanner, bringing the pulley into the centreline of the engine to allow the belt to be removed. There is no tension adjustment on items like the compressor or alternator, all tension being via just one tensioner.

There is no conventional distributor and coil on these engines. Instead individual coils sit underneath

The coils have to be removed to gain access to the spark plugs. Sometimes small amounts of oil will be found inside the spark plug area, mostly on the left-hand side because of spillage when topping up the oil level. A tip: if oil is found here yet the surrounding area is very dry, this could mean that the spark plug boss seals have been weeping slightly and need changing.

Spark plugs for these engines are conventional but expensive and they can be removed with a normal

Underneath the covers of the V8 engine, the coils are revealed with their neat wiring. (Nigel Thorley)

spark plug socket. The gap should be around 1.2mm, but there have been many changes over the years, so check with your particular handbook first.

Moving on we come to the air filter, which sits in a box at the front of the engine bay. Undoing a quite fragile breather pipe and five clips (one of which is difficult to access and requires the removal of a duct) the box can be opened and the disposable filter removed.

While in the engine bay, you should carry out a visual check of all areas to look for leaks, seepages, or anything that looks untoward. It is also a good idea to clean off any loose debris and dust. It is all too common for owners not to visually check the engine oil level between the 10,000-mile service intervals. There can, however, be unseen oil leaks that need to be checked and rectified. For example, take the style of cam cover gaskets used today. Although quite heavy duty, and sitting in ridges within the cam covers, as they get older the ridges can start to crack so the gaskets don't seat correctly and oil can leak out.

Finally, on internal servicing issues, move back to the rear of the vehicle. The battery in the boot is not normally of the 'sealed for life' type so care should be taken when topping up to avoid spillage. Acid could soon damage the boot floor or surrounding wiring.

Now the external checks. Radio aerial masts tend to stick. Unlike many modern cars, XKs still use a mast on the rear wing that raises and retracts as the audio system is turned on and off. The mast should be raised and regularly cleaned with WD40; do *not* use oils or grease, because these will attract dirt and eventually stop the mast from moving. Even using WD40 the mast should be wiped clean afterwards.

A visual check of all lights should be carried out, replacing the bulbs as necessary, none of which present any major problems (relevant information is provided in the handbooks).

It has, in the past, been normal practice to replace the windscreen wiper blades at 10,000-mile service intervals. Although Jaguar's policy on this has changed now, they should still be checked, and for the sake of the minimal cost involved the blades should be replaced both for safety reasons and to avoid unnecessary damage to the screen.

Last but not least, and again not identified in the normal Jaguar schedule, all door locks, hinges, etc. should be cleaned and oiled.

Access for the air cleaner element, a disposable item. (Nigel Thorley)

Variable valve timing

The normally aspirated AJ-V8 engines fitted to the XK range are equipped with variable valve timing, which produces the best idle quality of any Jaguar engine, the timing altering throughout the rev range. The solenoids to control this fit on the outside of the engine, fed from the ECU via a relay. You can occasionally get rattling noises from a build-up of coked oil. By disconnecting a multi-pin connector, you can apply 12 volts to ensure they move properly. Do not confuse this noise with a rattling timing chain tensioner or chain.

The throttle body of a V8 engine removed, showing the butterfly-style plates (arrowed) which will gum up and cause problems. (Nigel Thorley)

The Autologic system from Diagnos.co.uk Limited is extremely useful (in some cases vital), if very expensive for the home mechanic. (Nigel Thorley)

Throttle bodies

Common running problems can often be attributed to the electronic throttle body on these engines, which is to some extent overly complex. Numerous sensors and overrides are built in to prevent problems such as over-revving. Cumbersome, and not the most reliable piece of equipment, there have been cases where an engine has stalled for no apparent reason, particularly when at speed. There has been an unofficial recall because of this, in which modifications have been made.

Throttle plates can gum up with carbon, causing them to stick. This also applies to the gears, causing erratic control of the throttle. If changing throttle bodies, it is vital to first disconnect the battery because of the new 'learning process' the system goes through when it is reconnected.

Emissions

XK engines are not prone to problems in this area. Normally, if substantial problems arise at MOT time, this can be put down to using the wrong petrol or damage to a catalytic converter.

Electrics

These are without doubt the most complex part of an XK and a totally different concept to the wiring in older cars. Some circuits transfer data along multiplexing lines, passing through several components that appear unconnected in their use or purpose, down the same wire but at different frequencies. As such the electrical system on XKs cannot always be measured in the conventional way by use of voltage meters.

In some cases these data circuits have series connections, which means if one wire or connection breaks then everything on that network could fail to communicate. This will lead to erroneous messages on the dashboard, which may result in error messages in the diagnostics that bear little resemblance to what has actually gone wrong. The gearbox selector switch is a common source of problems, as by misuse or rough handling these switches can become dislodged or break. If a break is determined via messages on the dashboard, this is a good place to start looking, being a common area of concern.

Engine fail-safe modes, 'limp-home', etc. can all often be attributed to a simple breakage in the system like this, and you can't pick up the fault by the use of fault codes as you could with cars like the XJ40 and XJ-S. Instead you need diagnosis from a computerised link using a system like Autologic, which can not only 'read' the car's electrics but can transform the data into lists of faults, identify areas to inspect, and provide solutions – all at a price which is normally too high for the home DIY mechanic to consider. Similar in basic format to the sophisticated systems used by Jaguar dealerships, more and more independent Jaguar specialists are now going down this route, so it is important to entrust such work to one of these in order to determine the true problems with a car.

Unfortunately, different mechanics having attempted to rectify problems over the years will, in itself, result in several pages of erroneous faults showing up on diagnosis. The only real answer, if the car is still drivable, is to cancel out all the faults on the readout, continue to use the car, and then download the latest information a few days later to give you a more viable starting point for repairs.

On a simpler note, the condition of the main battery is crucial to good running. If it is in a poor state or is not of the correct size and power for the car, all sorts of faults can occur which can even affect engine running.

It is worth pointing out here, for the benefit of owners who don't read or remember items from their handbook, that the XK8 models are currently unique in Jaguar terms in having side windows that move up and down as the doors are opened and closed. This is done to ensure an efficient seal of the window glass edge with the rubber seal to reduce wind noise in both Convertible and Coupé models, as the side windows are frameless.

Whenever the battery is disconnected or goes flat, the system memory on the windows will fail and has to be reset. This is done by turning on the ignition and lowering each window fully, keeping the appropriate button pressed all the time until a 'click' is heard, then repeating the same operation with the window going up until they 'click'.

If indicators or other lights don't work, this can often be down to broken wires. The wiring looms are tightly attached to the steering column and can come apart at multi-pin connectors. To get to this area you may have to remove the steering wheel and airbag assembly. The airbag should *never* be tampered with – there are adequate warnings on the reverse, and if the bag inadvertently went off it could cause severe damage.

All the electrical signals affecting the steering wheel controls and the airbag pass through a cassette at the top of the column. If a fault occurs, the cassette will need changing. Incidentally, an airbag fault warning may also be down to high resistance caused by this cassette.

Air conditioning

All XKs were equipped with air conditioning as standard equipment, essentially the Nippon Denso system also fitted to corresponding XJ saloons. This is generally reliable, but will only work as efficiently as the cooling system as a whole, for which see the appropriate section above. The vulnerable part is the condenser situated at the front of the car, which is manufactured from light alloy and gets covered in debris as a result of its location. It also deteriorates naturally with age.

Interior temperature sensors can also give trouble. The ambient temperature is measured from outside, underneath the front bumper. Inside the car, a sensor sits adjacent to the boot-lock opening button in the dash liner. Over time, dust and dirt gather inside this, insulating it from temperature changes and thereby compromising the efficiency of the whole air conditioning system. It can be easily cleaned and reused. Simply pull the dash liner down from its clips to get at it.

Other problems can occur with the heater electric scavenge pump and electric control valve. This pump is especially for the cooling and heating system, and is designed to ensure that coolant passes through the matrix at a controlled rate. Both components can fail. If

A diagrammatic view of the air conditioning layout. (Nigel Thorley)

the valve fails, this normally shows up in the form of cold air and no heater. If the pump fails, when engine speed is above 2,500rpm one tends to get a degree of air inside the car due to high water pump speeds forcing coolant through the matrix. Changing these components is not easy. The pump, for example, is situated above the gearbox and a catalyst on the left-hand side has to be removed for best access.

A lot of common problems associated with air conditioning really relate to lack of proper usage. It is advisable to thoroughly read the instruction manual supplied with the car to familiarise oneself with how the system operates.

Trim

Generally speaking the trim is much more durable on these cars than on Jaguar models from the 1970s and 1980s. However, with the greater use of plastics and other lightweight materials, they only appear fine until disturbed, so great care should always be taken when prising off trim panels and removing clips, fasteners and cables, etc.

As already mentioned several times, take extreme care with wiring. Some wires are gathered together in clusters or intertwined and can easily get dislodged from their connections or damaged. Wires can also corrode easily with the advent of any damp, even inside their insulation.

A 'before and after cleaning' comparison of typical air conditioning components, which gather debris over a period of time.
(Nigel Thorley)

Accessing equipment like the radio control unit involves the removal of the whole centre console. The retaining clips around the gear select often break and then a replacement panel will be required.

Instrument illumination bulbs can be problematic. Although not over-complicated to deal with, a considerable number of different bulbs (over 30) are used in the dashboard and centre console area. They may look the same, but they are all very different wattages and replacing them with the wrong bulbs can either cause overheating or can have a negative effect on other illuminations. Replacing bulbs in the dashboard area requires the removal of the wood-veneered panels. These are merely veneered onto aluminium substrates, some of which are clipped onto the dash area. The central small gauge unit will just prise off, but the main instrument surround is secured by two screws at its base. Various fasteners and screws allow the main instrument pack to be removed, the same applying to the central auxiliary gauges (non satnav-equipped cars), which are removed as one complete unit.

Hood problems

Back in 1987 the then new XJ-S Convertible used a type of hydraulic fluid in the rams to pull the hood up and down electrically without problem, but with the introduction of the XK8 model in 1996 Jaguar opted to change the type of fluid. However, the new type was later found to gel, which caused the hood to open and close either very slowly or, at worst, stopped it entirely, obliging the electrical system to shut down to avoid unnecessary damage.

Although initially put down to insufficient hood use in certain countries (such as the UK) or to cold temperatures, it eventually became clear that this fluid was just not suitable for sustained use. Jaguar now use Pentosin CHF 11S fluid in all Convertibles, and this is what you should use to replace the fluid in earlier cars.

To do this the old fluid has to be completely purged from the system, to avoid contaminating the new fluid. This requires accessing all the areas of concern, and you must start with the hood in the retracted position. If this can't be done via the hydraulics, it can be

To carry out the fluid change in an XK Convertible the top screen rail and trim must be removed to access the pipes and latch-box. (Nigel Thorley)

The jelly-like substance formed by the old fluid, which has to be purged from the system. (Nigel Thorley)

The boot-mounted pump which also has to be disconnected from its mounting to purge the old fluid. (Nigel Thorley)

manually unlatched by means of the Allen key found in the boot area. Access is also required to the top screen rail inside the car, which requires removing the sun visors, trimmed panel, roof lighting panel, and top and side upholstered panels, and disconnecting the electrics. A substantial strengthening frame has to be undone, which gives access to the hood latching mechanism. Eventually the top rail can be withdrawn from its position revealing, on its left side, the pipes that run the fluid from the pump at the back of the car to the latching mechanism.

The pipes need to be carefully prised from the rail and disconnected so that the rail can be removed completely. The old fluid is then purged by a combination of bleeding the pipes to the latch-box inside the car and bleeding the hood hydraulics. This is done by electrically operating the hood several times and continually draining off the fluid, and manually operating the latch-box several times to extract the old fluid from it and its adjoining connections. The pump then has to be removed from its mounting in the boot and, with its filler plug removed, inverted to allow all the fluid in the reservoir to drain out (being careful not to let any run into the boot or onto the surrounding trim).

Refilling with new fluid and temporarily remounting the pump, the hood mechanism is powered up whilst containers collect the fluid as it is expelled from the disconnected pipework inside the car. This can take some time, as the old gelled fluid creates quite a resistance. Often compressed air is required to clear

A new bumper-bar mounting fitted to a car and well greased to guard against future corrosion. (Nigel Thorley)

the pipes out individually. Once the pipes to the latch-box are clear, they can be reattached to the flushed latch-box and reassembled. Now the hood must be operated at least two or three times, draining off the fluid after each operation.

It goes without saying that the utmost care and cleanliness should surround these operations to avoid contamination of trim and, of course, the pump mechanism and piping.

Rear bumper mountings

It is quite common for the mountings of the rear bumper bar on XK models to corrode badly, eventually leading to departure of the bumper bar! This is down to the mounting bracket, which is made from a form of glass-reinforced fibre composite plus an alloy stud with steel insert, which corrodes. The only answer is to change the mounting brackets, which are not costly, and then protect the components by the liberal use of copper grease to prevent similar problems in the future.

On the assumption that the bumper hasn't dropped off there are under-rear-wing closing panels to be removed to gain access to the bolts. These will probably be seized in position anyway, and it is probably best to prise away the bumper as by this time little is holding it in place. In many cases a brass ferrule in the bumper will seize and eventually become dislodged, which will need re-gluing in position and even tapping out to reclaim the thread.

Keeping your XK clean and presentable

Following most of the information above will give you a good grounding in what to look for and how to look after these cars. After this it is down to you, the owner, to fettle the car to ensure it stays in shape.

Cleaning the exterior is something many leave to the power-wash at their local garage, but there is a lot more you can do to keep your XK in top condition. The first thing to remember – and I keep plugging this point – is that the XK8 is very much based on XJS technology as far as the body and floorpan are concerned, and this spells the word 'care'. If you regularly and personally wash your car, look out for the telltale signs of corrosion starting, and stone chips that will allow damp to corrode the metal underneath.

Modern paintwork is more robust than in the past but it still benefits from care and attention, so polish the exterior once a year with a good quality wax. Every two to three years, for a regularly used example, the paintwork will benefit from 'cutting back' to remove road grime and minor scratches, followed by a good polish to bring the shine and brightness back.

Tips on doing this work start with good preparation. That means wear clothing without exposed buttons, and not wearing jewellery or having anything else on you that is likely to scratch the paintwork accidentally. Thoroughly wash and dry the paintwork to remove any loose dirt and grime before the main work begins. It is always worth taking care of other parts of the car (just in case); for example, if it is a Convertible, cover the hood and even the glass areas for protection, and always remove the wiper blades, because if cutting or buffing paste gets into the blades they could seriously scratch your windscreen afterwards. The use of cutting paste should be minimal, one panel at a time, in a rotational action and without being heavy-handed. A non-orbital electrical polisher can be used, but they need to be handled carefully and lightly so as not to buff too far into the body of the paint. Also be aware that trailing electrical cables can scratch your car.

Using clean cloths and operating in a circular motion, polish each panel, removing the remains of the cutting compound. Then polish the car using a good quality wax, again working on small areas at a time and moving in a circular motion so as not to leave streaks in the paintwork.

The final result is gratifying, and it is satisfying to the eye to keep your XK as good, if not better, than when it left the factory.

Modifications and miscellanea

It is amazing to know what has been and is currently being offered in the way of enhancements and accessories for the XK. Jaguar themselves have, from the very beginning, offered a range of interesting (and sometimes useful) accessories, and after about 1999 outside companies also started to take a keen interest in the car, initially offering accessories or aesthetic add-ons but subsequently expanding into major styling changes and mechanical/performance enhancements.

Factory accessories

Let's firstly take a look at what Jaguar had to offer, ignoring the merely cosmetic items and personal 'accessories'. Ignoring the R-Performance options brochures and lists, there have been no less than ten

If you're looking for period factory-supplied accessories for your XK, there is plenty of choice in this incredible range of brochures. (Nigel Thorley)

specific 'Accessory' publications from Jaguar (the first in July 1996, updated in a larger format at launch in October), offering a diverse range of useful items from a small 14-piece attaché case Tool Kit to an Inclination Sensor to detect unauthorised jacking/towing of the vehicle. One of the more useful safety products was Alpha Dotting, the microscopic particle implant of the vehicle's identification number at various locations around the car.

Useful items to avoid damage to trim included a hard preformed ABS protective liner for the boot, a soft tailored boot mat, and washable nylon fitted covers for the front seats. A very useful accessory was plastic headlamp covers to protect them from stone chips and cracking, a similar item being available for early fog lamps as well.

Right from the beginning Jaguar offered a range of luggage fitments for the XK, from a boot-lid mounted rack (with or without an aerodynamic matching suitcase) to ski-holders and bike-holders. Jaguar even offered a range of fitted suitcases for the boot (none of which were very popular because of the cost), ranging from a set of five traditional vulcanised black cases with straps to six soft fabric and leather cases or even seven rigid equivalents (not all of which fitted in the boot!).

Incredible to think, but yes, all these suitcases were made to – and do – fit in the boot of an XK8, providing you have a space saver! (Nigel Thorley)

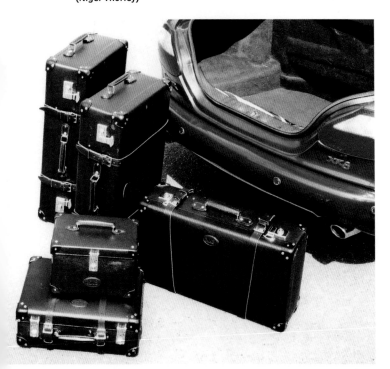

The 1998 catalogue followed the same format as the car brochures with virtually the same range. A new lockable Security Box was now available, which fitted in the boot to hold valuables like passports and jewellery when in transit, and luggage retainers for the boot floor could be added. An add-on Satellite Navigational System (CD-based) could now also be after-market fitted, with the remote screen sited to the right of the driver in front of the fresh air vent.

Yet another brochure in 1999 heralded a revised range. Now the accessory Tool Kit was in the form of a zip case and came with a pair of gloves, and there was a Front Bonnet Protector, a vinyl cover to guard against stone chips. Jaguar also offered the Star TAC 130 mobile phone system, with a phone unit fitted in the centre console storage area. By this time Reverse Park Sensing had become an after-market fit as well.

2000 saw yet another brochure but offered a reduced range of accessories for the XK. For colder climes an Engine Block Heater was now listed. From 2001 an Auxiliary Power Socket could be fitted in the glovebox or boot, ideal for charging mobile phones, for example.

By 2004 the range of items had been dramatically reduced and, indeed, the brochures now covered most Jaguar models. Entirely new for the XK were items like an all-wood rim steering wheel and an improved range of storage and sports holding equipment.

Alloy wheels

The choice of factory-supplied alloy wheels has been extensive and sometimes confusing. The initial supply gave buyers the option, during build or after-market, of the 18in Flute or a chromed plate 17in Revolver. Alternatively, but rarely seen, there was the option of the XJR's 17in five-spoke, exposed nuts, wheel. Another rarity, offered for most of the XK's production life, was winter-quality tyres fitted to conventional steel wheels (with plastic hubcaps à la X-300).

As the deletions and additions to the alloy wheels range were extensive over the years it is easiest to present them by year with accompanying pictures, which will be found in Appendix C. Suffice at this point to say that nearly all the wheels listed are interchangeable between models, though this may depend on the fitment of uprated brakes and other issues.

R-Performance

The introduction of R-Performance options from 1999 provided a wider choice for XK owners. Essentially the products available covered improved brakes and handling packages with a new range of alloy wheels. However, various items were an only-fit with selected other products from the range. For example, the uprated Brembo brakes could only be fitted with one of the larger alloy wheel sets. Initially the alloy wheel range was made up of the 18in BBS Milan, 20in BBS Paris and 20in BBS Detroit, and at this stage a new Winter Tyre was offered fitted to an open 10-spoke alloy wheel.

From 2001 a new 20in Montreal wheel was offered, and in 2002 Recaro sports seats with soft grain leather, matching steering wheel and gear knob, and even an Aluminium Pack with instrument surrounds, foot pedals and gear lever surround. In 2004 the R-Performance took a more extravert approach, with an expansive brochure covering its availability for all Jaguar models. For the XKs specifically another 20in split-rim alloy wheel was added to the range, the Sepang.

Outsiders

Outside companies started to take an interest in the Jaguar XK8 in 1999. Paramount Performance, for example, were already promising a wide range of options, many of which came from the German Arden Company. Arden themselves introduced a 460bhp version of the XKR which also took some styling cues from the XK180. Called the A-type, this had a carbon

fibre body, remapped electronics, race-tuned exhaust system and lowered suspension, along with further weight savings. Suggested top speed was in the region of 190mph, with 0–60mph acceleration time of 4.5 seconds. Six pot callipers on the front wheels and four pot at the rear improved the braking system. Externally the reformed body panels gave the car more aggression, as did the wider mouth at the front and new lighting treatment all round.

Since that time Paramount Performance, and now Racing Green and others, have progressed further, with a whole range of options to bring cars up to particularly high performance standards, with enhanced trim and styling. Literally anything is available.

How to improve the looks of your XK

If you have or expect to purchase an XK there is so much you can do without going to the extremes of some of the Paramount and Racing Green projects. It is all down to how much money you want to spend and what type of car you want to end up with.

For example, let's take wheels again. If you don't like the wheels that Jaguar offered there is still plenty of choice, providing you take care to ensure the wheels

A typical Paramount Performance 'Grand Prix' XKR with many of their improvements included, providing over 400lb ft of torque. (Nigel Thorley)

More changes to the exterior with new lighting treatment at the rear, in this case from Racing Green. (Courtesy Racing Green Ltd)

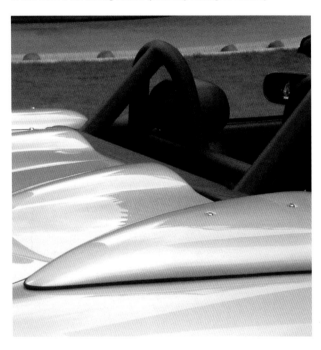

For the ultimate improvement to a Convertible, this torpedo effect aluminium tonneau cover can be finished to any body colour and fits neatly behind the rear seat when the hood is erect. (Courtesy Racing Green Ltd)

you buy will actually fit. Paramount, Racing Green and even local companies can offer a wide range of wheels to suit your requirements. S.N.G. Barratt from Shropshire in the UK, well-known Jaguar parts supplier, offer a range of Dayton wire wheels from the USA for XK models of various types. Supplied as a bolt-on fit, no special temporary or permanent adaptations are required on the existing XK hubs. The wheels are built

Fancy a nose job? Any colour, most shapes, take your pick from the many after-market alternatives available. (Nigel Thorley)

to a high quality to take the stress to which a modern and relatively heavy car like the XK can subject them. They are chrome plated and any existing 18in tyres can be fitted to them. All you have to remember is that they are more difficult to clean than conventional wheels!

If you want to substantially change the look of your XK's interior, then this can also easily be changed in varying degrees. All offer a range of options, from individually chosen wood veneer with unique grains to Piano Black finishes and even high contrast upholstery/trim options. Seats can even be re-trimmed

Could something like this be a 'warp' too far for some XK owners? It's all down to personal taste! (Courtesy Paramount Performance)

If you are looking for a bit more veneer and something different to leather, then how about this door trim? (Courtesy Paramount Performance)

Or go all the way and have the seats re-upholstered as well. (Courtesy Paramount Performance)

And let's not forget the rear, where you can do almost as much as you can at the front! (Nigel Thorley)

It is perfectly possible to fit brighter bulbs to upgrade the lighting in the XK without xenon systems. (Nigel Thorley)

to suit, and you can accommodate upgraded sound systems and alarms, etc.

How to improve safety and comfort

Reverse park aids can be fitted to cars that predate the availability of such systems from Jaguar or its dealerships. Widely available from many outlets, after-market kits like the 'Third Eye' can be fitted easily and safely. The general principle is that sensors fitted to the rear bumper face are activated when reverse gear is selected. A signal beam senses obstacles at a preset distance and emits an intermittent 'bleep', the bleeps getting more frequent the closer the car gets to the obstacle(s).

The advantage of a four-sensor rear parking system is that it provides the extra spread required to cover all eventualities when reversing. (Nigel Thorley)

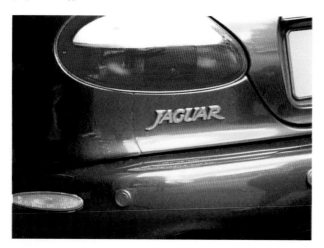

Prices will vary for these kits, which are in the main cheaper than buying direct from a Jaguar dealership. It is important, in view of the width of the XK, to select a kit with *four* sensors, not two or three – four will provide a good spread of beam. Each kit comes complete with detailed instructions.

After measuring up to ensure the sensors are correctly positioned as shown in the kit instructions, the bumper can be drilled. Take care not to damage surrounding paintwork. The sensors and their housings will be clearly different from one another and marked as such: it is vital that they are fitted as instructed so that the beams can function correctly.

Feed the wires through into the boot area (which may involve removing some of the boot trim), where the system's control box/pick-up unit must be mounted. This has to be connected to one of the car's reversing light circuits, as it will pick up the signal when reverse is selected and the reversing lights come on. The other wire from the pick-up unit goes to the audible warning bleeper, which has to be accommodated somewhere inside the car.

Reed Automotive is one company offering headlight bulb upgrades for non-xenon equipped XKs. Under the names Silverstone and Cool Blue, they claim the bulbs dramatically improve light output with up to 50 per cent more light on the road.

Brake-dust shields are now available for most Jaguar alloy wheels for the XK, from inexpensive rubber types through to well-fitting metal types – Kleen Wheels for example, offer grooved shields which have a heat sink property to dissipate heat. As well as the safety advantage of keeping brakes cool, these also improve the longevity of alloy wheels by dispersing the dust created from the brake pads.

At the other extreme of safety devices Jaguar Products now even produce specially made roll-over cages for the XK, so we may soon see examples on the tracks alongside the XJSs, XJ Saloons and XK/E-type sports cars which participate in the Jaguar Enthusiasts Club Series.

Jaguar never produced a hard top for the Convertible XK models so this was left to outside contractors. Both Arden and LS Design produced examples, the latter made from a double-skinned shell of glass fibre fitted with Velour or leather trim. Cost when new was around £5,500, dependent on trim finish.

Classic Additions offer a range of after-market items for XK models. From fitted indoor or outdoor car covers in various colours, they progressed to producing stainless steel mesh grilles and wind deflectors for the Convertibles, which turned out a lot cheaper than the Jaguar-supplied item.

If you don't have an XK already equipped with a satnav system, you might consider SmartNav from Traffic-master. It is a specialist fit (and is now recommended by Jaguar themselves), with nothing on show inside the car except for a small screen (if you want it). Otherwise you just have a button that connects you directly to their control centre and you simply voice request your requirements, which are

The Arden hardtop for XK Convertibles isn't cheap and can be difficult to store when not on the car. (Courtesy Paramount Performance)

downloaded to your car and then voice directions are given. As a 'real time' system it even keeps track of traffic conditions and informs you accordingly, changing your route when necessary.

How to improve performance

Various companies have produced, and still continue to produce, a range of enhanced exhaust systems for XK

Classic Additions provide this wind deflector, ideal for keeping the ladies' hair still when the top is down. (Nigel Thorley)

One of the many after-market exhaust systems available for the XK, this one a Tiger system from Double S. (Courtesy Double S Exhausts)

models. At AJ6 Engineering, ex-Jaguar man Roger Bywater has for some time been producing performance enhancements for many different Jaguar models. He claims around 20bhp improvement in performance (and sound) with his XK8 modified stainless steel system. Double S Exhausts supply a very lightweight, lifetime-guaranteed stainless steel system

with improved gas flow and a choice of over 30 tailpipe options. Elite & Performance from Derby also offer a range of exhaust options. Their handcrafted 'RR' systems use aircraft grade stainless steel, factory moulds to ensure a perfect fit, and free flow silencers for enhanced performance, and offer two levels of sound output, 'Road Sport' and 'Track Sport'. Paramount Performance and Racing Green also offer a vast range of exhaust options for all XK models – the choice is endless.

Torque Developments offer a range of engine management upgrades. This includes a modified induction system for the XK8 which smoothes out the airflow, minimising restrictions of incoming air, aiding performance and economy. The system comes complete with replacement filters and pipework clips and unions for ease of installation.

This is also another area where companies like Racing Green and Paramount can help with all sorts of options, from improving airflow to increasing the supercharger speed. An interesting adaptation they have to enhance the steering feel is the ability to change from lighter to slightly stiffer steering dependent on driving conditions. The system is relatively inexpensive to fit, is operated by a simple button on the dash or centre console, and certainly does improve the feel.

The XK lends itself to a whole range of options for exhaust systems, many of which follow the original lines so don't hang lower, with a choice of pipe diameter to create more or less sound as the owner requires. This conversion was carried out by Elite & Performance of Derby (Nigel Thorley)

Torque Developments offer such performance improvements as a modified induction system. (Torque Developments)

In addition the same companies offer a steering-wheel based paddle-gearchange system, something other manufacturers (and finally Jaguar) have also adopted. Still allowing operation via the conventional J-gate, changes up and down the 'box can be made by simply pressing a button on the steering wheel.

For budding home-mechanics, with the finance and expertise, and specialist Jaguar independent garages working on XKs these days, the Autologic diagnostics system is a notebook-sized casing with its own integrated 12in colour touch screen that utilises solid-state technology and connects to the car's own interior multi-pin socket, from where the Autologic unit also gets its power. It has the ability to download and upload information from the Diagnos.co.uk website, providing quick and easy access to expertise when a problem needs attention. This also means any changes in the software can be made quickly and efficiently. The equipment can provide valuable services such as modifying the engine management systems, programming other electronics and even reprogramming key-fobs – just like a Jaguar dealership diagnostic system.

Lastly, if you don't want to improve the momentum performance of your XK, you can certainly improve the fuel consumption dramatically with an LPG alternative fuelling system. These are getting more sophisticated all the time, the price of LPG is still significantly below that of petrol, and with modern techniques it is easy to fit a system without losing too much space in the boot, although you will have to resort to a can of tyre sealant instead of a spare.

As you can tell, there is so much to go at for the XK

It is feasible to fit an LPG conversion to an XK. (Nigel Thorley)

models and more is being offered as time goes on. You can choose to keep your XK as original as it left the factory, or can make it truly individual – the choice is yours. If, however, you want something really different that won't affect your 'real' car, then how about an XK8 pedal car, made by Pedal Power of Middlesex? An engined version was also available, equipped with Honda four-stroke 83cc unit producing about 2hp. It had two forward gears, reverse, and a clutch, and could supposedly reach 15mph. And if that proved too expensive, there were and still are plenty of XK8 and XKR models and toys around!

The XK8 children's car, powered and suitable for ages up to about ten – without a licence! (Nigel Thorley collection)

There are still plenty of XK models around, from simple plastic toys to highly detailed die-casts in most common scales. (Nigel Thorley collection)

Chapter Eleven

People and cars

And finally, a few more images of XKs, some unusual and some belonging to famous or infamous people.

Where all the Bond 'special' vehicles were prepared. Unfortunately the XKRs used Ford power! (Nigel Thorley collection)

Perhaps the best-known XK of them all, from the James Bond Movie *Die Another Day*. Unfortunately the XK belonged to the bad guy, while Mr Bond enjoyed his usual Aston Martin. (Nigel Thorley collection)

Austin Powers 'Shaguar' look-alikes turn up everywhere, even today.
(Nigel Thorley collection)

Well-known singer Gabrielle has an XK. (Jaguar Cars Limited)

And it isn't only pop stars that get cars like XKs. Here Clive Woodward OBE, the sportsman, receives his new XKR. (Jaguar Cars Limited)

And we mustn't leave out footballers like England's Michael Owen. (Jaguar Cars Limited)

Lino Pires (right) of The Butcher's Arms and Tony Robin from The Dining Room, well-known chefs with their Jaguars. (Jaguar Cars Limited)

XKs are regularly used for charity raisers like this run to Scotland and back for the NSPCC. (Nigel Thorley)

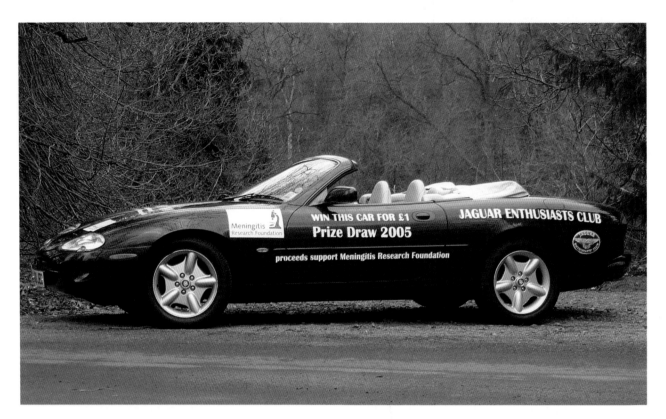

And the Jaguar Enthusiasts Club annually gives away an XK8, the funds raised for various charities. (Nigel Thorley)

And for something entirely different, this is the XK-RS produced by Rocketsports in the US to commemorate their race wins with XKs. (Rocketsports)

Going racing

Competitive activity has always been important in building the reputation of Jaguar Cars, the company making a name for itself in both rallying and racing even though its later diversion into Formula One proved a disaster. At the time of writing, no one has yet assumed a competition mantle for the XK – no one,

that is, except Paul Gentilozzi of Rocketsports, from Michigan in the USA.

Gentilozzi formed the Rocketsports organisation in 1985, since when it has grown into a major player in engine development and race car preparation, and an incredibly successful competitor in the American Trans-Am race series, which Jaguar had participated in years before with Bob Tullius and his Group 44 team in an E-type and later an XJ-S.

Rocketsports initially built three Jaguar XKRs with carbon fibre and Kevlar bodies and, to compete, used Ford V8 engines. Jaguar has always provided some support for the team, which in the earlier years involved prizes for the drivers, the end of season lucky recipient getting the key to a new XKR.

By April 2003 no less than eight XKRs were racing in the Series, each one pumping out in the region of 700bhp. The cars took four of the top six places in just the first few months of the season. At this time the cars were still fitted with powerful Ford V8 engines, but later in that season the 4.2-litre supercharged AJ-34 was substituted, heavily modified by Rocketsports, who bored it out to 4.5 litres to produce 650bhp in un-supercharged form with a massive 425lb ft of torque,

The Rocketsports XKRs make a phenomenal sight and sound in the US races, and long may their success continue. (Rocketsports)

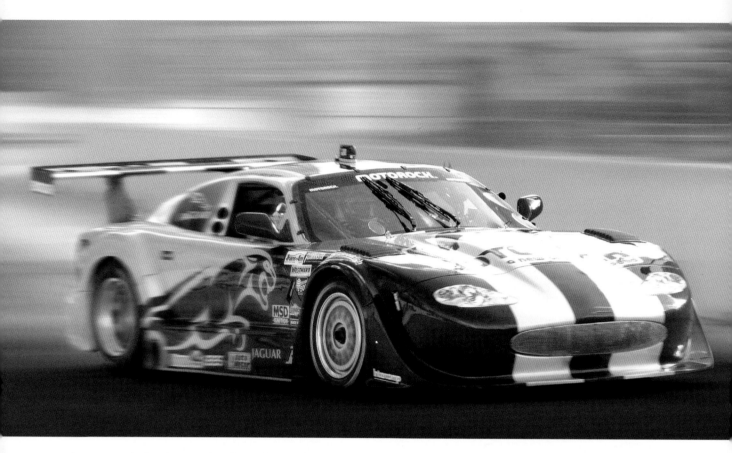

Awesome, as the Americans put it – what a sight! (Rocketsports)   This says it all – Long live the XK! (Nigel Thorley)

revving to around 9,000rpm. For strength, the crankshaft was replaced with a more substantial one with lightweight racing pistons and con rods, and Rocketsports adopted the Bosch MS3.3 fuel injection system and a custom-made manifold. Their quoted performance figures are a top speed of around 180mph and a 0–60mph time of a mere 3.2 seconds!

By the end of 2003, with eight wins out of ten race starts, the Trans-Am Championship was Jaguar's, secured at the last race by a stunning 1–2–3. The Championship had been won for Jaguar twice before, back in 1978 by the old Group 44 team driving an XJ-S, and in 2001 with another XKR under Ford power, and

the Rocketsports team would go on to win again in 2004 – an even more resounding victory, their fourth in total – when XKRs accounted for four out of the top six positions in the Championship.

The same racing team developed their own high-performance concept car based on the XK, called the XK-RS, first shown at the Las Vegas Speciality Equipment Manufacturers Show in 2004. Using wind-tunnel testing to achieve a true ground effects package, and uprated styling for an even more aerodynamic approach, the expansion of the AJ-34 engine to 5.0 litres and 550bhp created a potentially 200mph XK.

Natural development from the XK8: the ALC Concept (2005) and the
new aluminium XK (2006 on). (Jaguar Cars Limited)

Production figures

	1995	1996	1997	1998	1999	2000	2001	2002	2003	2004	2005	Totals
XK8 Coupé	8	2,925	5,141	3,319	1,701	1,514	1,723	1,203	985	627	602	19,748
XK8 Convertible	12	4,187	9,765	7,662	6,196	5,907	4,404	2,910	2,280	2,003	1,434	46,760
XKR Coupé	–	–	11	1,402	1,530	1,778	1,659	1,053	936	708	584	9,661
XKR Convertible	–	–	12	838	1,994	3,042	2,949	1,695	1,455	1,075	835	13,895
Totals	20	7,112	14,929	13,221	11,421	12,241	10,735	6,861	5,656	4,413	3,455	90,064

Specifications

	XK8 4.0 Coupé	XK8 4.0 Convertible	XKR 4.0 Coupé	XKR 4.0 Convertible
cc	3996	3996	3996	3996
Bore (mm)	86	86	86	86
Stroke (mm)	86	86	86	86
Compression ratio (to 1)	10.75	10.75	9	9
bhp (@ rpm)	290 @ 6100	290 @ 6100	370 @ 6150	370 @ 6150
Max torque (lb ft @ rpm)	290 @ 4250	290 @ 4250	387 @ 3600	387 @ 3600
Automatic transmission	ZF 5-speed	ZF 5-speed	Mercedes 5-speed	Mercedes 5-speed
Wheel size (std) front	8in x 17in	8in x 17in	8in x 18in	8in x 18in
Wheel size (std) rear	8in x 17in	8in x 17in	8in x 18in	8in x 18in
Braking system	Ventilated discs, ABS, split circuits, park brake on rear	Ventilated discs, ABS, split circuits, park brake on rear	Ventilated discs, ABS, split circuits, park brake on rear	Ventilated discs, ABS, split circuits, park brake on rear
Steering	Rack & pinion variable ratio	Rack & pinion variable ratio	Rack & pinion variable ratio	Rack & pinion variable ratio
Steering turns lock to lock	2.8	2.8	2.8	2.8
Turning circle	36ft 2in	36ft 2in	36ft 2in	36ft 2in
Suspension (front)	Independent unequal length wishbones, steel coil springs, telescopic dampers, anti-roll bar	Independent unequal length wishbones, steel coil springs, telescopic dampers, anti-roll bar	Independent unequal length wishbones, steel coil springs, telescopic dampers, anti-roll bar, Adaptive Technology	Independent unequal length wishbones, steel coil springs, telescopic dampers, anti-roll bar, Adaptive Technology
Suspension (rear)	Independent double wishbone driveshafts acting as double links, concentric steel springs, dampers, anti-roll bar	Independent double wishbone driveshafts acting as double links, concentric steel springs, dampers, anti-roll bar	Independent double wishbone driveshafts acting as double links, concentric steel springs, dampers, anti-roll bar, Adaptive Technology	Independent double wishbone driveshafts acting as double links, concentric steel springs, dampers, anti-roll bar, Adaptive Technology
Top speed	155mph	154mph	155mph	155mph
0–60mph acceleration	6.4 seconds	6.7 seconds	5.2 seconds	5.3 seconds
Average fuel economy	22.9mpg	23.3mpg	22.5mpg	22.2mpg
Overall length (mm)	4760	4760	4760	4760
Overall width (mm)	1829	1829	1829	1829
Overall height (mm)	1296	1306	1296	1306
Wheelbase (mm)	2588	2588	2588	2588
Unladen weight (kg)	1615	1705	1640	1750
Front track width (mm)	1504	1504	1504	1504
Rear track width (mm)	1498	1498	1498	1498
Boot volume (litres)	327	307	327	307
Fuel tank capacity (litres)	75	75	75	75

	XK8 4.2 Coupé	XK8 4.2 Convertible	XKR 4.2 Coupé	XKR 4.2 Convertible
cc	4196	4196	4196	4196
Bore (mm)	86	86	86	86
Stroke (mm)	90.3	90.3	90.3	90.3
Compression ratio (to 1)	11	11	9.1	9.1
bhp (@ rpm)	300 @ 6000	300 @ 6000	400 @ 6100	400 @ 6100
Max torque (lb ft @ rpm)	310 @ 4100	310 @ 4100	408 @ 3500	408 @ 3500
Automatic transmission	ZF 6-speed	ZF 6-speed	ZF 6-speed	ZF 6-speed
Wheel size (std) front	8in x 19in	8in x 19in	9in x 20in	9in x 20in
Wheel size (std) rear	9in x 19in	9in x 19in	9in x 20in	9in x 20in
Braking system	Ventilated discs, ABS, split circuits, park brake on rear	Ventilated discs, ABS, split circuits, park brake on rear	Ventilated discs, ABS, split circuits, park brake on rear	Ventilated discs, ABS, split circuits, park brake on rear
Steering	Rack & pinion variable ratio	Rack & pinion variable ratio	Rack & pinion variable ratio	Rack & pinion variable ratio
Steering turns lock to lock	2.8	2.8	2.8	2.8
Turning circle	36ft 2in	36ft 2in	36ft 2in	36ft 2in
Suspension (front)	Independent unequal length wishbones, steel coil springs, telescopic dampers, anti-roll bar	Independent unequal length wishbones, steel coil springs, telescopic dampers, anti-roll bar	Independent unequal length wishbones, steel coil springs, telescopic dampers, anti-roll bar, Adaptive Technology	Independent unequal length wishbones, steel coil springs, telescopic dampers, anti-roll bar, Adaptive Technology
Suspension (rear)	Independent double wishbone driveshafts acting as double links, concentric steel springs, dampers, anti-roll bar	Independent double wishbone driveshafts acting as double links, concentric steel springs, dampers, anti-roll bar	Independent double wishbone driveshafts acting as double links, concentric steel springs, dampers, anti-roll bar, Adaptive Technology	Independent double wishbone driveshafts acting as double links, concentric steel springs, dampers, anti-roll bar, Adaptive Technology
Top speed	155mph	155mph	155mph	155mph
0–60mph acceleration	6.1 seconds	6.3 seconds	5.2 seconds	5.3 seconds
Average fuel economy	24.9mpg	24.7mpg	22.9mpg	22.6mpg
Overall length (mm)	4776	4776	4776	4776
Overall width (mm)	2015	2015	2015	2015
Overall height (mm)	1296	1306	1296	1306
Wheelbase (mm)	2588	2588	2588	2588
Unladen weight (kg)	1685	1775	1735	1815
Front track width (mm)	1504	1504	1504	1504
Rear track width (mm)	1498	1498	1498	1498
Boot volume (litres)	327	307	327	307
Fuel tank capacity (litres)	75	75	75	75

Alloy wheel ranges

Style	1996	1997	1998	1999	2000	2001	2002	2003	2004	2005
17in Revolver	X Std XK8	X	X	X	X	DCL	–	–	–	–
17in Revolver Chrome	X	DCL	–	–	–	–	–	–	–	–
18in Flute	X	X	X	X	X	DCL	–	–	–	–
17in Sport (XJR)	X	X	X	X	DCL	–	–	–	–	–
18in Double Five	–	–	–	X Std XKR	X	X	X	X	X	DCL
17in Lamina	–	–	–	–	–	X Std XK8	X	DCL	–	–
18in Impeller	–	–	–	–	–	X	X	DCL	–	–
17in Gemini	–	–	–	–	–	–	–	X Std XK8	X	X
18in Hydra	–	–	–	–	–	–	–	X Std XKR	X	X
18in Centaur	–	–	–	–	–	–	–	X	X	DCL
19in Apollo	–	–	–	–	–	–	–	X	X	X Std Prem XK
18in Aris	–	–	–	–	–	–	–	–	–	X Std R Prem/S
17in Winter Steel	X	X	X	X	X	X	X	X	DCL	–
18in Winter Alloy	–	–	–	X	X	X	X	X	X	X
18in Milan (R-Per)	–	–	–	X	X	X	X	DCL	–	–
20in Paris (R-Per)	–	–	–	X	X	X	X	X	DCL	–
20in Detroit (R-Per)	–	–	–	X	X	X	X	X	X	X
20in Montreal (R-Per)	–	–	–	–	–	–	–	X	X	X
20in Sepang (R-Per)	–	–	–	–	–	–	–	–	X	X

DCL = Discontinued Line

Revolver

Revolver Chrome

Flute

Sport

Double Five

Lamina

Impeller

Gemini

Hydra

Centaur

Apollo

Aris

Winter Steel

Winter Alloy

Milan

Paris

Detroit

Montreal

Sepang

Suggested maintenance schedule

Work	10,000 miles	20,000 miles	30,000 miles	40,000 miles	50,000 miles	60,000 miles	100,000 miles	Other
Replace engine oil, filter and sump washer	X	X	X	X	X	X	–	–
Visual check for fluid leaks	X	X	X	X	X	X	–	–
Inspect brake pads (rotor condition on change)	X	X	X	X	X	X	–	–
Replace air cleaner element (normally aspirated)	–	–	X	–	–	X	–	–
Replace air cleaner element (supercharged)	–	X	–	X	–	X	–	–
Replace fuel filter	–	–	–	–	–	X	–	–
Replace spark plugs	–	–	X	–	–	X	–	–
Check drive belt tension wear indicator	X	X	X	X	X	X	–	–
Renew drive belt (normally aspirated)	–	–	–	–	–	–	X	–
Renew supercharger drive belt	–	–	–	X	–	–	–	–
Grease drive shaft universal joints	X	X	X	X	X	X	–	–
Check brake fluid level	X	X	X	X	X	X	–	–
Check coolant level and specific gravity	X	X	X	X	X	X	–	–
Check windscreen washer reservoir level	X	X	X	X	X	X	–	–
Check battery electrolyte level	X	X	X	X	X	X	–	–
Check power steering fluid level	X	X	X	X	X	X	–	–
Replace windscreen wiper blade rubbers	X	X	X	–	X	X	–	–
Replace windscreen wiper blades	–	–	–	X	–	–	–	–
Check condition of all tyres, pressures, etc	X	X	X	X	X	X	–	–
Oil door locks, hinges, wax protect brake/fuel lines	X	X	X	X	X	X	–	–
Check lights, horn and other electrics	X	X	X	X	X	X	–	–
Replace gearbox oil and filter	–	–	–	–	X	–	–	–
Renew coolant, flush radiator and check hoses	–	–	–	–	–	X	–	–
Replace brake fluid	–	–	–	–	–	–	–	2 or 4 years
Road test	X	X	X	X	X	X	–	–

The above are based not only on normal franchised dealer schedules but also experience, and therefore include extra items not necessarily covered by the Jaguar dealerships.

Exterior colour schemes

Notes
* Indicates not available on XKR models in that year.
+ Indicates only available on the XKR model for that year.

	1996	1997	1998	1999	2000	2001	2002	2003	2004	2005
Spindrift (white)	X	X	X	X*	X	–	–	–	–	–
White Onyx	–	–	–	–	–	X	X	X	X	X
British Racing Green	X	X	X	X	X	X	X	X	X	X
British Racing Green (metallic)	–	–	–	–	–	–	X	X	X	X
Emerald (dark green)	–	–	–	–	X	X	–	–	–	–
Aquamarine	X	X	X	–	–	–	–	–	–	–
Sherwood (mid green)	X	X	X	–	–	–	–	–	–	–
Alpine (mid green)	–	–	–	X*	X	–	–	–	–	–
Seafrost (pastel green)	–	–	–	–	X	X	X	X	X	X
Sapphire (dark blue)	X	X	X	X	X	X	–	–	–	–
Westminster (dark blue)	–	–	–	–	X	X	–	–	–	–
Antigua (mid blue)	X	X	X	X	–	–	–	–	–	–
Pacific (mid blue)	–	–	–	–	X	X	X	X	X	X
Adriatic (mid blue)	–	–	–	–	–	–	X	X	–	–
Amaranth (purple)	–	–	X	X	–	–	–	–	–	–
Ultraviolet (purple)	–	–	–	–	–	–	–	–	X	X
Ice Blue (pastel)	X	X	–	–	–	–	–	–	–	–
Zircon (pastel blue)	–	–	–	–	–	–	X	X	X	X
Mistral (blue/grey)	–	–	–	–	X	X	–	–	–	–
Titanium (grey)	X	X	–	–	X	X	X	–	–	–
Meteorite (silver)	–	–	X	X	–	–	–	–	–	–
Platinum (silver)	–	–	–	–	X	X	X	X	X	X
Quartz (dark grey)	–	–	–	–	–	–	X	X	X	X
Slate (dark grey)	–	–	–	–	–	–	X	X	X	X
Anthracite (black)	X	X	X	X	X	X	–	–	–	–
Ebony (black)	–	–	–	–	–	–	X	X	X	X
Midnight (black metallic)	–	–	–	–	–	–	X	X	X	X
Topaz (gold)	X	X	X	X	X	X	X	X	X	X
Roman Bronze	–	–	–	–	–	X	–	–	–	–
Carnival (dark red)	X	X	X	X	X	X	X	X	–	–
Phoenix (red)	–	–	–	X+	X	X	X	X	–	–
Salsa (red)	–	–	–	–	–	–	–	–	X	X
Radiance (darker red)	–	–	–	–	–	–	–	–	X	X
SPECIALS										
Copper Black (S/Victory models)	–	–	–	–	–	–	–	–	–	X
Frost Blue (S/Victory models)	–	–	–	–	–	–	–	–	–	X
Bay Blue (S/Victory models)	–	–	–	–	–	–	–	–	–	X
Satin Silver (S/Victory models)	–	–	–	–	–	–	–	–	–	X
Jupiter Red (Portfolio models)	–	–	–	–	–	–	–	X	–	–
Coronado Blue (Portfolio models)	–	–	–	–	–	–	–	X	–	–

Trim colour schemes

	1996	1997	1998	1999	2000	2001	2002	2003	2004	2005
SPORT MODELS										
Oatmeal Leather/Charcoal Facia	X	X	X	X	X	X	X	–	–	–
Charcoal Leather/Charcoal Facia	X	X	X	X	X	X	X	X	X	X
Cream Leather/Charcoal Facia	X	X	–	–	–	–	–	–	–	–
Oatmeal Cloth/Charcoal Facia	X	X	X	X	X	–	–	–	–	–
Charcoal Cloth/Charcoal Facia	X	X	X	X	X	–	–	–	–	–
Ivory Leather/Charcoal Facia	–	–	X	X	X	X	X	X	X	X
Nimbus Leather/Charcoal Facia	–	–	–	–	X	X	X	–	–	–
Dove Leather/Charcoal Facia	–	–	–	–	–	–	–	X	X	X
Heritage Tan Leather/Charcoal Facia	–	–	–	–	–	–	–	X	X	–
Cranberry Leather/Charcoal Facia	–	–	–	–	–	–	–	X	X	–
Heritage Tan/Charcoal Leather/Charcoal Facia	–	–	–	–	–	–	–	X	X	–
Cashmere Leather/Sable Facia	–	–	–	–	–	–	–	–	–	X
Ivory Leather/Sable Facia	–	–	–	–	–	–	–	–	–	X
CLASSIC MODELS										
Oatmeal Leather/Antelope Facia	X	X	X	X	X	X	X	–	–	–
Cream Leather/Sable Facia	X	X	–	–	–	–	–	–	–	–
Charcoal Leather/Charcoal Facia	X	X	X	X	X	X	X	X	X	X
Teal Leather/Dark Teal Facia	X	X	X	X	–	–	–	–	–	–
Cashmere Leather/Sable Facia	–	–	X	X	X	X	X	X	X	X
Ivory Leather/Sable Facia	–	–	X	X	X	X	X	X	X	X
Nimbus Leather/Slate Facia	–	–	–	–	X	X	X	–	–	–
Dove Leather/Charcoal Facia	–	–	–	–	–	–	–	X	X	X
Heritage Tan Leather	–	–	–	–	–	–	–	X	X	–
Cranberry Leather	–	–	–	–	–	–	–	X	X	–
Heritage Tan/Charcoal Leather/Charcoal Facia	–	–	–	–	–	–	–	X	X	–
Cranberry/Charcoal Leather/Charcoal Facia	–	–	–	–	–	–	–	X	X	–
Ivory Leather/Charcoal Facia	–	–	–	–	–	–	–	–	–	X
DASH TRIMS										
Stained Maple/Birds Eye Maple	X	X	X	X	X	X	X	X	X	X
Burr Walnut Veneer	X	X	X	X	X	X	X	X	X	X
Elm	–	–	–	–	–	–	–	–	X	–
Piano Black	–	–	–	–	–	–	–	–	–	X
HOOD COLOURS										
Black	X	X	X	X	X	X	X	X	X	X
Stone	X	X	X	–	–	–	–	–	–	–
Blue	X	X	X	X	X	X	X	X	X	X
Green	X	X	X	X	X	X	X	X	X	X
Dark Beige	–	–	X	X	X	X	X	X	X	X
Light Beige	–	–	–	X	X	X	X	X	X	X

Appendix G

UK sales brochures

Year	Models	Cover	Description	Pages	Identity code
1996	XK8	Black/Red car nose	'The Cat is Back' Abridged teaser with reply form	6	JLD/10/22/21/96
1996/7	XK8	Black/Blue car nose	'The Cat is Back' Full launch brochure with developments pics, specs, etc	50	JLD/10/01/21/96
1996/7	AJ-V8 engine	Green	'Refined Power' Engine launch information		
1997	XK8	Blue portrait with sea	Range brochure including X-300 saloons	28	JLD/10/02/00.96.1
1998	XK8	Cream landscape	Range brochure including V8 saloons	32	JLD/10/02/00/98
1998	XK8	Green square	XK range brochure with new pics	36	JLD/10/01/21/98
1998	XKR	Red nose	XKR launch brochure	14	JLD/10/01/36/98
1999	XK8/R	Cream/Red car	XK range brochure, revision of XKR launch and 1998 green XK8 brochures	44	JLM/10/02/03/99
2000	XK8/R	Blue/Black bonnet	XK range, major revision of previous XK brochures	44	JLM/10/02/03/00
2000	S'stone	Mesh grille	Loose-leaf portfolio to celebrate XKR Silverstone special edition model		
2001	XK8/R	Green, car at speed	XK range revision	50	JLM/10/02/03/01
2001	XKR100	Green R-Performance	XKR/XJR 100 special edition large portrait format fold-out card		JLM/10/02/14/02
2001	XK8/R	Green 'Art of Performance'	XK/XJ Range brochure, square format, poster at rear		JLM/10/01/00/01
2002	XK8/R	Four car line-up	XK/XJ/X/S range brochure, A5 landscape format	32	JLM/10/15/00/02
2002	XK8/R	Four car line-up	Revision of above	32	JLM/10/15/00/02.5
2003	XK8/R	Silver XKR nose	XK range brochure, large portrait format, separate colour chart	62	JLM/10/02/03/03
2003	XK8/R	Silver XKR nose	Abridged version of above	24	JLM/10/20/03/03
2003	XK8/R	Silver, inset pictures	XK/X/S/XJ range brochure, A5 landscape format	24	JLM/10/15/00/03
2004	XK8/R	Black XK at speed	New style range brochure	50	JLM/10/02/03/54
2004	XKR400	Black box sleeve	Prestige XKR400 special edition	34	J4849
2005	XK8/R	Black XKR	New style range brochure with sleeve	40	JLM/10/02/03/04.5
2005	Carbon Fibre	Black with holes	Carbon Fibre prestige limited edition brochure with sleeve	42	J5213
2005	4.2 S	White/oilskin sleeve	Luxury hardbound brochure	40	JLM/10/02/04/06
2005	XK8/R	Black	'Born to Perform' XK/XJ/S/X range brochure	52	JLM/10/15/00/05

The above does not include special brochures prepared for markets outside the UK.

A p p e n d i x **H**

XK specialists

This list is purely a guide and should not be considered as definitive or, indeed, a recommendation of the work carried out. It is merely a list of known specialists of the models covered in this publication. Obviously, it does not include the many Jaguar franchised dealerships, nor does it cover the many specialists outside of the UK.

Anybody contemplating placing work should first ensure the company or individual has the expertise and equipment necessary to carry it out, get a reasonable estimate of the cost and time involved, and, ideally, get references from other XK enthusiasts who may have used them.

International clubs

There are numerous small organisations around the world catering for the Jaguar marque, many of which are one-country or area based. For example, in the USA and Australia a single organisation oversees and co-ordinates the work of many small regional Jaguar clubs.

Jaguar Clubs of North America (JCNA). An organisation formed to bring together the 50 or more small clubs and organisations in the States looking after 6,000 Jaguar enthusiasts. For more details contact: JCNA, c/o Nelson Rath, 1000 Glenbrook, Anchorage KY 40223, USA. E-mail: nrath@jcna.com. Website: www.jcna.com.

Australian Council of Jaguar Cars. Eight smaller Jaguar clubs in Australia, all of which can be contacted through the *Australian Jaguar* magazine. Council e-mail: info@jagqld.org.au.

Jaguar Enthusiasts Club. Based in the UK, this is the world's largest Jaguar marque club, with over 20,000 members worldwide (with local regional get-togethers). It caters for all Jaguar models but has a particularly strong XK8 and XKR membership. As well

as an award-winning full colour, 108 page glossy monthly magazine (free to members), the Club also boasts the JagAds website for the sale and purchase of cars and parts, many national and international events, shows, tours, a regular XK seminar, an XK8 Forum website, and even the hire and sale of specialist tools. It also carries the largest available range of Jaguar merchandise including clothing and books, and has a special Club-specific car insurance scheme. Jaguar Enthusiasts Club, Abbeywood Office Park, Emma Chris Way, Filton, Bristol, South Gloucestershire, BS34 7JU. Tel: 0117 9698186. E-mail: jechq@btopenworld.com. Website: www.jec.org.uk.

Jaguar Drivers Club. The oldest UK Jaguar club, offering external and social events for all Jaguar owners including XKs. A monthly glossy magazine is supplied free to members, and a range of merchandise is available. Jaguar Drivers Club, 18 Stuart Street, Luton, Bedfordshire, LU1 2SL. Tel: 01582 419332. Website: www.jaguardriver.co.uk.

The XK8 Enthusiasts Club. A fairly new and small one-man business set up to look after the interests of XK owners with a quarterly newsletter, helpful advice and an annual XK event. XK Enthusiasts Club, 2 Lynton Road South, Gravesend, Kent, DA11 7NF. Website: www.xkec.co.uk.

Monthly magazines with regular XK content

Jaguar Driver. Organ of the Jaguar Drivers Club (see above), and free on subscription to the club. 86 pages.

Jaguar Enthusiast. Organ of the Jaguar Enthusiasts Club (see above), and free on subscription to the club. 108 pages, full colour with regular articles, including technical, on the XK range, extensive classified advertisements, parts for sale, etc.

Jaguar Heritage. Published in conjunction with the Jaguar Daimler Heritage Trust. Offers excellent quality colour photography, and historical information relating to all things Jaguar. Website: www.jaguarheritagemag.com.

Jaguar World Monthly. The only other regular Jaguar monthly magazine available on the UK High Street. Comprehensive coverage of all things Jaguar. Contact Kelsey Publishing. Tel: 01959 541444. Website: www.jaguar-world.com

Brochures, handbooks, press releases and other paperwork

Jaguar Daimler Heritage Trust. Maintaining all the factory records and information on behalf of Jaguar Cars Limited, they can supply (for a fee) a wide range of information, photographs, etc, relating to the XK models. From time to time they also have various press releases, brochures, etc, for sale, and now produce a range of CD-roms covering paperwork, maintenance information, etc, for XKs. Jaguar Daimler Heritage Trust, c/o Jaguar Cars Limited, Browns Lane, Coventry, CV5 9DR. Tel: 02476 202141. Website: www.jdht.co.uk.

Andrew Swift. Well-known enthusiast and collector of written matter relating to the Jaguar marque. He can supply all manner of specialist paperwork on the XK models and other Jaguars. Andrew Swift, 56 Greystone Avenue, Sheffield, South Yorkshire, S11 7AZ. Tel: 0114 2685158.

Sales, servicing, other maintenance and enhancements

Arun Limited, Codmore Hill Garage, Stane Street, Pulborough, West Sussex, RH20 1BQ. Tel: 01798 874477. E-mail: sales@arunltd.com. Pre-owned Jaguar XK sales.

Chiltern of Bovingdon, Chesham Road, Bovingdon, Hertfordshire. Tel: 01442 833311. E-mail: sales@chilternltd.co.uk. Pre-owned Jaguar car sales.

Classic Additions, Stert, Devizes, Wiltshire, SN10 3JD. Tel: 01380 720419. E-mail: sales@classicadditions.co.uk. Range of after-market accessories such as mesh grilles, car covers and wind deflectors.

David Manners Limited, 991 Wolverhampton Road, Oldbury, West Midlands, B69 4RJ. Tel: 0121 544 4040. Website: www.davidmanners.co.uk. Major supplier of new parts for all Jaguars, including some XK items.

David Marks Garages, Unit 36, Nottingham South & Wilford Industrial Estate, Nottingham, NG11 7EP. Tel: 0115 982 2808. E-mail: david@davidmarksgarages.co.uk. Modern Jaguar service and other maintenance. Any work carried out from 10,000-mile service to engine changes. Technical expert advice supplied to the Jaguar Enthusiasts Club.

Diagnos.co.uk Limited, Cuxham Road, Watlington, Oxfordshire, OX49 5NB. Tel: 01492 614300. Website: www.diagnos.co.uk. Suppliers of specialist Autologic software and hardware suitable for XK models.

Dorset Jag Centre, Bailie Gate Industrial Estate, Sturminster Marshall, Dorset. Tel: 01258 858541. Website: www.dorsetjagcentre.co.uk. Pre-owned Jaguar XKs for sale, plus service and maintenance and breakdown recovery.

Elite & Performance Limited, Unit 10, Derby Trading Estate, Stores Road, Derby, DE21 4BD. Tel: 01332 265826. Website: www.eapj.com. Modern Jaguar service plus brake, suspension and engine upgrades, uprated exhaust systems and body kits.

Eurojag, Sovereign House, Neasham Road, Hurworth Moor, Darlington, Co. Durham, DL2 1QH. Tel: 01325 722777. Website: www.eurojag.com. Jaguar dismantlers including accident-damaged XK8s.

Jaguar at Beechdown, Beechdown Garage, Totnes Road, Paignton, Devon. Tel: 01803 520026. Website: www.beechdownjaguar.com. Pre-owned Jaguar XKs for sale.

Jagutek, 22 Lancaster Way Business Park, Ely, Cambridgeshire, CB6 3NW. Tel: 01353 667147. Website: www.jagutek.co.uk. Modern Jaguar servicing plus new and used parts.

Kent Jaguar Centre, Unit 1, Hillside Farm, Rushmore Hill, Knockholt, Sevenoaks, Kent, TN14 7NL. Tel: 01959 533305. Modern Jaguar servicing and diagnosis and parts supply.

Kings Road Garage, 1 Kings Road, Berkhamsted, Hertfordshire, HP4 3BD. Tel: 01442 863851. Website: www.kingsroadgarage.co.uk. Pre-owned Jaguar XK car sales.

Les Pauls Jaguar Specialists, 300/302 Chigwell Road, Woodford Green, Essex, IG8 8PN. Tel: 020 8505 5055. Website: lespaulsmotors.co.uk. Pre-owned Jaguar car sales, service and maintenance including air conditioning.

Lodsworth Garage, Collyers Yard, Lickfold, Petworth, West Sussex, GU28 9DT. Tel: 01798 861356. E-mail: ron@lodsworthgarage.com. Modern Jaguar service, air conditioning service and repair.

Myrtle Productions, 2 Wilbrough Road, Birchington, Kent, CT7 9DY. Tel: 01843 844962. E-mail: myrtleprod@aol.com. Website: www.myrtleprod.com. Range of upgraded interior woodwork, steering wheels and gear knobs for the XK range.

Nene Specialist Cars, 8 Harvester Way, Fengate, Peterborough, Cambridgeshire, PE1 5UT. Tel: 01733 349042. Website: www.nenejags.co.uk. Modern Jaguar service, maintenance and diagnosis including air conditioning, wheel alignment, etc.

NM Jags, Mendip Garage, A37 Gurney Slade, Radstock, Somerset, BA3 4UU. Tel: 01749 840864. Website: www.nmjags.co.uk. Pre-owned Jaguar XKs for sale plus servicing.

Paragon Design, Unit 4, Bure Valley Business Centre, The Street, Lammas, Norfolk, NR10 5AF. Tel: 01603 279027. E-mail: sales@paragondesignuk.com. Website: www.paragondesignuk.com. Range of body kits for XK range.

Paramount Performance, STS House, Bristol Way Business Park, Stoke Gardens, Slough, Berkshire, SL1 3QB. Tel: 01753 571759. Website: www.paramount-performance.com. Extensive range of upgrades for the XK from body kits, exhausts, and lights to drive train enhancements and performance options.

Racing Green Limited, Station Road West, Ash Vale, Hampshire, GU12 5QD. Tel: 01252 894773. Website: www.racinggreencars.com. Extensive range of upgrades and enhancements for XK models, from new interior woodwork, body kits, and exhausts, to major performance changes.

S&P Auto Services, Unit 3 Haywood Estates, Pottery Road, Kingsteignton, Newton Abbot, Devon, TQ12 3BN. Tel: 01626 369551. Website: www.thejaguarspecialists.co.uk. Modern Jaguar service and pre-owned car sales.

Simon March & Co, Scoreby Lodge, Hull Road, Dunnington, York, YO19 5LR. Tel: 01904 489821. Modern Jaguar service and maintenance.

S.N.G. Barratt Group, Bridgnorth, Shropshire, WV15 6AP. Tel: 01746 765432. E-mail: sales.uk@sngbarratt.com. Website: www.sngbarratt.com. Major suppliers of new parts, including some XK items.

Specialised Automotive Services, Clitheroe, Lancashire, BB7 9EQ. Tel: 01282 776081. E-mail: sasservicesltd@talk21.com Website: www.sas-automotiveservices.co.uk. Special XK number plate plinths and grilles.

Surrey Jag Centre, 91 Canterbury Road, Croydon, Surrey, CRO 3HH. Tel: 020 8689 3333. Website: www.surreyjag.co.uk. Modern Jaguar service and diagnosis.

Wyn Thomas, Unit 1, Eppingdene, Ivy Chimney Road, Epping, Essex, CM16 4EL. Tel: 01992 571532. Website: www.wyn-thomas.co.uk. Pre-owned Jaguar XKs for sale plus service and maintenance.

XJ Motor Services, The Brooks, Lyne Lane, Lyne, Chertsey, Surrey, KT16 0AW. Tel: 01932 564441. Website: www.xjmotorservices.com. Modern Jaguar servicing, refurbished alloy wheels.

Index